Woman's Day
Chocolate LOVERS' Cookbook

Woman's Day
Chocolate LOVERS' Cookbook

by Marlene K. Connor
& the Editors of *Woman's Day*

CROWN PUBLISHERS, INC.

NEW YORK

Copyright © 1984 by CBS Publications, Inc.
Published by Crown Publishers, Inc., One Park
Avenue, New York, New York 10016, and simulta-
neously in Canada by General Publishing Compa-
ny Limited
WOMAN'S DAY and logo are trademarks of CBS Publi-
cations, Inc.
Manufactured in the United States of America

Library of Congress Cataloging in Publication Data
Connor, Marlene K.
Woman's day chocolate lovers' cookbook.
Includes index.
1. Cookery (Chocolate) I. Woman's day.
II. Title.
TX767.C5C66 1984 641.6'374 83-27219
ISBN 0-517-55191-8
10 9 8 7 6 5 4 3 2 1
First Edition

Contents

The Joys of Chocolate: An Introduction

Chocolate. This hauntingly rich flavor is America's favorite passion. What childhood hasn't been filled with crispy, golden chocolate-chip cookies and fresh ice-cold milk, chocolate bars that once cost a nickel or Grandma's scrumptious chocolate layer cake? As we grow up we continue to enjoy these pubescent joys while our palates become alert to new, more sophisticated treats. The satisfying chocolate pudding that was a frequent family dessert becomes heavenly chocolate mousse with dollops of fresh whipped cream; the chocolate candy bar that was so inexpensive becomes designer chocolates in gold boxes that are such an investment we're afraid to eat them; and Grandma's irresistible chocolate layer cake . . . well, that will always be just the same—the best ever.

The joy of chocolate never ends, thank goodness. Chocolate has the uncanny ability to be light and delicate in a perfect soufflé or gloriously dark and decadent in a chocolate-pecan torte. It can make you feel absolutely wicked while dipping fresh fruits or bits of cake in a bubbly fondue or guilty when sneaking another bite of chewy home-baked fudge.

Now, *Woman's Day*, the most trusted name in cooking and baking, presents this delicious assortment of fine chocolate recipes. This varied collection was chosen with both the beginner and expert cook in mind. The classic chocolate treats are all here along with some of the elegant desserts you thought you'd never make at home.

Here is an endlessly rich array of cakes, pies, cookies, brownies, desserts, drinks, and confections—the stuff that sweet dreams are made of—all filled with wholesome ingredients. We've selected the best recipes which will supply you with an endless choice of chocolate desserts. *Woman's Day*'s expert cooks and testers offer this tribute to chocolate's versatility. It will surely become a classic cookbook in any kitchen library.

A Bit of Chocolate History

Chocolate and its close kin, cocoa, actually grow on trees, in a manner of speaking. Both chocolate and cocoa are made from beans of the cacao tree, which is a native of hot, humid forests of the Amazon basin. These trees grow in many parts of the world, but flourish only in countries close to the equator. Of course, they can now be cultivated under controlled conditions.

Chocolate can be traced as far back as when Christopher Columbus brought it to Spain after his trip to the New World. Chocolate was the royal drink of the Aztec Indians. They enjoyed it flavored with spices, but it was consumed cold and unsweetened. It is not known how long the Aztecs had been enjoying this delicious flavor, but it was not until the invasion of Cortez in 1519 that the use of chocolate was finally recorded. Cortez, sensing that chocolate would be a source of income in Spain, learned the cultivating process from the Aztecs. He then reintroduced chocolate to Spain as a hot drink, where sugar and vanilla flavor were added. It didn't take very long for chocolate to become extremely popular, and the Spaniards held on to the processing secret for nearly a hundred years.

In the middle of the 1600s when the Spanish princess Maria Theresa married Louis XIV, the French began to enjoy the richness of chocolate as well. At the same time, cocoa began to be cultivated in the British West Indies, and there were chocolate shops all over Europe where drinks were consumed by the gallon. It became quite fashionable to sip and gossip over a hot cup of chocolate.

In early 1700, chocolate was introduced to Americans in an interesting way. In 1765, a wealthy doctor, Dr. James Baker, financed the first chocolate factory in America. Dr. Baker had a very interesting use for chocolate. He ground it up and used it in medicines to improve their taste. The word "confection" actually described medicine that was flavored with spices, sugar, or chocolate. Today, of course, medicine is the last thing we think of when we talk of confections.

It wasn't long before chocolate was used in cooking. All sorts of baked goods were enhanced with its deep, rich flavor. Two innovations were still to occur with chocolate. The first can be credited to Daniel Peter, a Swiss, who decided to enjoy his chocolate with milk, thus creating the ever-popular *milk chocolate*. Another Swiss developed a process of creating smoothness in chocolate. Swiss chocolate remains the premium chocolate available today.

Chocolate has survived the centuries. Its ability to comfort, satisfy, and excite is what makes it one of America's favorite treats.

The Different Types of Chocolate

Chocolate's versatility has a lot to do with chocolate's ability to be processed into different forms. Here's a breakdown of those forms and their uses.

UNSWEETENED CHOCOLATE

This is the basic chocolate, the beginning of all the other chocolates. It is available in block form and is the natural, rich chocolate ground from the cacao bean. It is unsweetened (actually bitter) and has a deep, full-bodied flavor that makes it perfect for baking.

SEMISWEET CHOCOLATE

As the name implies, this chocolate has been slightly sweetened with sugar, some cocoa butter, and flavorings. It has a satin gloss when melted, making it particularly good for dipping, frostings, sauces, candy, and general baking.

SWEET COOKING CHOCOLATE

This chocolate has a higher amount of sugar (usually more sugar than chocolate) but is similar to semisweet chocolate. It is also called German sweet chocolate.

CHOCOLATE PIECES

These pieces of semisweet chocolate are also called bits, morsels, or chips. They contain sugar, cocoa butter, and flavorings, and retain their shape in baking. They are especially good in cookies, but can be found in ice cream, brownies, and happy mouths.

MILK CHOCOLATE

This chocolate is sweetened with sugar and contains powdered milk and other flavors. Milder and lighter than chocolate without milk, it is extremely popular in candy bars and is used primarily as an eating chocolate.

Other Chocolate Products

INSTANT COCOA

This combination of sugar, powdered milk, and other flavorings is used to make hot chocolate (or hot cocoa). Some forms of instant cocoa also dissolve in cold liquids, making it an ideal treat for children. But it is not suitable for cooking because it does not contain enough rich chocolate.

CHOCOLATE SYRUP

This is semisweet syrup (not to be confused with the pure chocolate "liquor" produced by grinding cacao beans) that contains sugar, cocoa, and corn syrup. It is used in baking and in beverages.

CHOCOLATY SUBSTITUTES

The "y" lets you know that the product does not contain any chocolate liquor. It gets its chocolaty flavor from a cocoa base with additional vegetable fats.

WHITE CHOCOLATE

White chocolate is not chocolate at all because it contains no cocoa. It is made with cocoa butter.

Cooking with Chocolate

HOW TO MELT CHOCOLATE CORRECTLY

Chocolate is a hardy ingredient to work with, but there are certain things that you must keep in mind. Since most chocolate recipes involve melting blocks of chocolate at some point, it is important to remember that chocolate burns easily and chocolate does not mix easily with moisture.

Begin by chopping the chocolate into equal-sized pieces. This will aid in even melting. It is best to use a double boiler. Allow the water to get very hot, but not boiling. Avoid water so hot that steam begins to rise; this steam might cause the chocolate to "tighten" and become a thick mass. Also, don't use a covered pot because the condensation from the lid might drip into the chocolate.

If your chocolate should tighten, all is not lost. You can soften it again by adding 1 or 2 tablespoons of solid vegetable shortening. Don't add butter or liquid vegetable oil; these contain moisture, which will also cause tightening.

Of course, you can melt chocolate in a saucepan directly over low heat, but it must be carefully watched, as chocolate burns quickly.

FAVORITE CHOCOLATE DECORATIONS

What is a French cream roll without chocolate shavings? What is a chocolate mousse without whipped cream? Garnishes make a dish more pleasing to the eye, but when they are made of chocolate they add to the flavor. Here are the secrets to creating those fabulous finishing touches.

Chocolate Shavings

Warm 1-ounce square (or whatever amount is needed) semisweet chocolate in palms. With swivel-bladed vegetable peeler pressed firmly against chocolate, move peeler toward you. Refrigerate shavings until needed.

Chocolate Curls or Shreds

With heavy-duty foil shape 3½ x 2½-inch foil pan; set aside. Melt 4 to 8 squares (1 ounce each) semisweet chocolate in top of double boiler over simmering water, stirring gently occasionally. Pour into foil pan. Smooth top; let stand at room temperature until firm, several hours or overnight. With slightly warmed swivel-bladed vegetable peeler or a thin-bladed sharp knife, shave chocolate bar lengthwise in thin slices to form curls. With spatula carefully transfer curls to cookie sheet lined with wax paper. Chill until firm. Store in covered container; use as needed as dessert garnish. Any leftover chocolate scraps can be remelted and reshaped into a smaller bar, then shaved as above. Or shred coarsely and use for garnish.

Chocolate Thins

Melt 2 squares (1 ounce each) semisweet chocolate. Pour onto cookie sheet lined with wax paper and spread in thin layer. Freeze until firm. With sharp knife cut in diamond or desired shapes. Return to freezer. Just before serving, carefully peel away wax paper. Use for garnish on dollops of whipped cream, cream pies, cakes, or ice cream. *Note:* Thins soften quickly at room temperature.

Thin Chocolate Rounds

Melt ½ cup (3 ounces) semisweet chocolate pieces over warm water; stir in ½ teaspoon vegetable shortening until smooth. Line baking sheet with wax paper; mark forty 1½-inch circles. In each circle place a rounded ¼ teaspoonful melted chocolate. Spread thinly within circle; refrigerate about 15 minutes or until chocolate sets. Peel rounds off paper; store covered in refrigerator or freezer. Use to decorate desserts. Makes 40.

Chocolate Wedges

Prepare chocolate and baking sheet as for rounds, marking four 4½-inch circles. Spread 1 rounded tablespoonful melted chocolate in each circle. Refrigerate 3 minutes or until chocolate just begins to set. Using knife, score each circle in 8 wedges. Chill until set. Proceed as above. Makes 32.

Whipped Cream

Beat 1 cup heavy cream and 2 tablespoons sugar until stiff. Serve. For chocolate-flavored whipped cream, add powdered unsweetened cocoa to taste while beating.

Storing Chocolate Properly

Chocolate stores very well and will be on hand when you have the urge to prepare something wonderful for dessert. But there are a few things to remember when storing your chocolate over a long period of time.

Chocolate should be stored in a cool, dry place at a temperature of about 60° F. If the chocolate does become warm, the fat will rise to the surface and give the chocolate a grayish film, which is called "bloom." If this happens, the chocolate is still perfectly edible or usable. But if the wrapper becomes oily, the chocolate has deteriorated. Although chocolate will last on a kitchen shelf or in the refrigerator for one year, it is best to keep *cooking* chocolate (which is likely to stay unused longer than *eating* chocolate) in the refrigerator where you're sure it won't melt easily. When storing chocolate in the refrigerator, allow it to return to room temperature before using.

All Kinds of Cakes

Baking a cake can be the most satisfying of all cooking experiences. So many wholesome ingredients go into the perfect layer cake that children enjoy simply licking the batter.

This chapter is filled with the cakes that you remember enjoying as a child along with many novelty cakes and sophisticated cakes that you might present at a special dinner party. This array of luscious chocolate cakes includes layer cakes, sheet cakes, sponge cakes, and a selection of creamy smooth cheesecakes. There is something here for every occasion from the classic Devil's Food Cake with Chocolate Shadow Icing to a French Chocolate Roll, a Sacher Torte, and a New York City Chocolate Cheesecake.

Cakes are the perfect dessert for special occasions such as birthday parties and anniversaries, or you can treat your family any night with a simple sheet cake or a pan full of cupcakes.

Grandma's Chocolate Cake

1 cup unsalted butter or margarine, softened

2 cups sugar

3 eggs, separated

3 squares (1 ounce each) unsweetened chocolate,
   melted and cooled

1¼ teaspoons active dry yeast

Water

2¾ cups sifted all-purpose flour

½ teaspoon salt

1 teaspoon baking soda

1½ teaspoons vanilla extract

Rich Mocha Frosting

Cream butter; gradually add sugar, beating until light and fluffy. Add egg yolks and beat until light. Blend in cooled chocolate. Dissolve dry yeast in ¼ cup warm water (105° to 115° F.). Add to chocolate mixture with sifted flour and salt. Beat egg whites until stiff; fold into mixture. Cover and let stand in warm place for about 4 hours.

Dissolve soda in 3 tablespoons hot water and add with vanilla to batter; beat well. Pour into three 9-inch layer-cake pans lined on bottom with greased wax paper.

Bake in preheated 350° F. oven 35 minutes. Cool, and frost with Rich Mocha Frosting.

Rich Mocha Frosting

Cream ¼ cup softened unsalted butter or margarine. Add 3 egg yolks and beat well. Add 4½ cups confectioners' sugar, ¾ cup cocoa, ¼ teaspoon salt, and 1 teaspoon vanilla extract. Gradually beat in enough strong coffee to give frosting spreading consistency.

Chocolate Shadow Cake

4 squares (1 ounce each) unsweetened chocolate
½ cup hot water
1½ cups sugar
½ cup unsalted butter, softened
1 teaspoon vanilla extract
3 eggs
2 cups sifted cake flour
1 teaspoon baking powder
½ teaspoon salt
⅔ cup milk
Buttercream Frosting
Chocolate Shadow

Melt chocolate in ½ cup hot water in top part of double boiler over hot water. Cook, stirring, until thickened. Add ½ cup sugar and cook, stirring, 2 to 3 minutes. Remove from water and cool.

Cream butter, then gradually add remaining sugar, and cream until light and fluffy. Add vanilla; add eggs one at a time, beating thoroughly after each. Add chocolate mixture and blend well. Sift together flour, baking powder, and salt, and fold into chocolate mixture alternately with milk, beginning and ending with flour mixture. Pour into two 9-inch layer pans lined on bottom with wax paper.

Bake in preheated 350° F. oven 30 to 35 minutes, or until cake tester comes out clean. Cool in pans 5 minutes, then turn out on cake racks to cool thoroughly. Spread frosting between layers and on top and sides of cake. Pour Chocolate Shadow over top, allowing some to run down sides of cake. Let chocolate set before cutting.

Buttercream Frosting

Beat together thoroughly ¾ cup softened unsalted butter, 2 egg yolks, and 1 teaspoon vanilla extract. Gradually add 2½ cups confectioners' sugar, beating until smooth.

Chocolate Shadow

Melt ½ cup semisweet chocolate pieces in top of double boiler over hot water. Blend in 3 to 4 tablespoons warm water, or enough to make mixture smooth and thin enough to pour.

Sour-Cream Chocolate Layer Cake

2 cups cake flour

1¼ cups sugar

1 teaspoon baking soda

1 teaspoon salt

1 cup sour cream

½ cup unsalted butter or margarine, softened

2 eggs

2 squares (1 ounce each) unsweetened chocolate,
  melted and cooled

¼ cup hot water

1½ teaspoons vanilla extract

Chocolate Cream Filling

Chocolate and Cream-Cheese Frosting

Chopped pecans

In large bowl of mixer stir together flour, sugar, soda, and salt. Add sour cream, butter, and eggs. Beat at low speed just until blended. Then beat at medium speed 2 minutes, scraping bowl occasionally. At low speed stir in chocolate. Add water and beat at medium speed 2 minutes more, scraping bowl occasionally. Stir in vanilla. Pour into 2 greased and wax-paper-lined 8-inch layer-cake pans.

Bake in preheated 350° F. oven about 25 to 30 minutes, or until pick inserted in center comes out clean. Cool on racks 10 minutes, then invert on racks, peel off paper, turn layers top sides up, and cool. Fill layers with Chocolate Cream Filling or your own favorite. Frost top and sides with Chocolate and Cream-Cheese Frosting or your own favorite. Decorate with pecans.

Makes 8 to 10 servings.

Chocolate Cream Filling

½ cup sugar

¼ cup flour

Dash of salt

1 cup milk

1 egg, slightly beaten

1 square (1 ounce) unsweetened chocolate

1 teaspoon vanilla extract

In small saucepan combine sugar, flour, and salt. Gradually beat in milk with small whisk. Cook and stir over medium heat until thickened and smooth. Remove from heat and beat in egg. While still beating, return to low heat for 30 seconds. Add chocolate and beat until melted. Beat in vanilla. Cut out a wax-paper circle to fit pan and place right on filling to keep skin from forming.

Chill. Stir before using.

Makes about 1½ cups.

Chocolate and Cream-Cheese Frosting

1 package (3 ounces) cream cheese, softened

2 tablespoons unsalted butter or margarine, softened

2 squares (1 ounce each) unsweetened chocolate,
    melted and cooled

Dash of salt

2½ cups unsifted confectioners' sugar

2 tablespoons half-and-half

1 teaspoon vanilla extract

In small bowl of mixer beat together cream cheese and butter until light and smooth. Stir in chocolate and salt. Add sugar alternately with half-and-half, beating thoroughly after each addition. Stir in vanilla.

Makes about 1⅔ cups.

Cherry-Chocolate Cake

6 eggs, separated

¾ cup sugar

1 teaspoon vanilla extract

½ cup cocoa mixed well with ⅓ cup flour

½ cup unsalted butter or margarine, melted and cooled

Cocoa Whipped-Cream Frosting

1 can (17 ounces) pitted dark sweet cherries, well drained,
  halved, then drained again

Chocolate Curls (page 8)

In large bowl of mixer beat egg whites at medium speed until soft peaks form. Increase to high speed and gradually beat in sugar until stiff peaks form; set aside.

Stir vanilla into egg yolks to break up and blend. Fold about one-quarter egg-white mixture into yolks; pour over remaining egg-white mixture. Sprinkle with cocoa mixture, a few tablespoons at a time, folding in gently but thoroughly after each addition. Fold in only clear part of melted butter, discarding milky residue. Divide batter evenly among 3 well-greased or paper-lined 8-inch layer pans.

Bake on center rack in preheated 350° F. oven 25 minutes, or until pick inserted in center comes out clean. Run small spatula around edge of layers, invert on racks, and peel off paper. Cool.

Prepare frosting. Remove 1 cup and fold in cherries; spread between layers, stacking. Frost top and sides of cake with remaining frosting. Decorate with Chocolate Curls. Chill at least 2 hours before serving.

Makes 8 to 10 servings.

Cocoa Whipped-Cream Frosting

In small bowl of mixer, mix well 4 tablespoons sugar with 3 tablespoons cocoa. Stir in 1½ cups heavy cream and ½ teaspoon almond extract. Chill with beaters at least 30 minutes. Whip until soft peaks form.

Makes enough to fill and frost three 8-inch layers.

Sweet-Chocolate Cake

4 squares (1 ounce each) sweet cooking chocolate
½ cup boiling water
1 cup unsalted butter or other shortening
2 cups sugar
4 eggs, separated
1 teaspoon vanilla extract
2½ cups sifted cake flour
1 teaspoon baking soda
½ teaspoon salt
1 cup buttermilk
Coconut-Pecan Filling
Chocolate Cream-Cheese Frosting

Melt chocolate in water; cool. Cream butter and sugar; add egg yolks, one at a time, beating thoroughly after each addition. Add vanilla and chocolate; mix well. Sift dry ingredients together and add alternately with buttermilk; beat until smooth. Fold in stiffy beaten egg whites. Pour into three 8- or 9-inch layer-cake pans.

Bake in preheated 350° F. oven about 35 minutes. Cool. Fill with Coconut-Pecan Filling and frost with Chocolate Cream-Cheese Frosting.

Makes 8 to 10 servings.

Coconut-Pecan Filling

In saucepan mix 1 cup undiluted evaporated milk, 1 cup sugar, 3 egg yolks, ½ cup unsalted butter or margarine, and 1 teaspoon vanilla extract. Cook, stirring, over medium heat for 12 minutes, or until mixture thickens. Add 1 cup flaked coconut and 1 cup chopped pecans. Beat until thick.

Chocolate Cream-Cheese Frosting

Cream 2 tablespoons unsalted butter and 4 ounces cream cheese; add 1½ squares (1½ ounces) melted unsweetened chocolate, dash of salt, 1½ cups sifted confectioners' sugar, ¼ cup heavy cream, and ½ teaspoon vanilla extract. Mix well.

Bavarian Chocolate Cake

2 cups fine, fresh pumpernickel bread crumbs (use firm bread
    with crust; make crumbs in blender)

⅓ cup light rum

4 squares (1 ounce each) semisweet chocolate, plus some
    extra chopped for garnish

⅓ cup walnuts

6 eggs, separated

1 cup sugar

1 teaspoon vanilla extract

Rum Whipped Cream

Sprinkle crumbs with rum and set aside. In blender grate 4 squares of chocolate and walnuts fine; set aside.

In large bowl of mixer beat egg whites at medium speed until soft peaks form. At high speed gradually beat in sugar until stiff, shiny peaks form. Stir vanilla into egg yolks until well mixed. Fold about one-quarter of egg-white mixture into yolk mixture, then pour over remaining egg-white mixture. Sprinkle with crumbs and chocolate-walnut mixture, folding in gently but thoroughly. Divide batter evenly among 3 greased 8-inch layer-cake pans lined with wax paper and greased again.

Bake in preheated 350° F. oven 30 minutes, or until pick inserted in centers comes out clean. Cool in pans on racks. Run a small spatula around edges, invert on racks, and peel off paper. Sandwich layers with about half the Rum Whipped Cream and frost with remaining half. Decorate with chopped chocolate. Chill overnight.

Makes 8 to 10 servings.

Rum Whipped Cream

In small bowl of mixer stir 1 to 1½ cups heavy cream, 3 tablespoons sugar, and 2 tablespoons light rum; chill at least 1 hour. Whip until soft peaks form (do not overwhip).

Diva Cake

1 cup unsalted butter or margarine, softened

1½ cups sugar

1 teaspoon vanilla extract

2 squares (1 ounce each) unsweetened chocolate,
   melted and cooled

5 egg yolks, well beaten

1½ cups sifted cake flour

1 teaspoon baking powder

¼ teaspoon baking soda

½ teaspoon salt

½ cup sour cream or buttermilk

2 tablespoons strong coffee

2 egg whites, beaten stiff

Brown-Sugar Frosting

Cream butter, sugar, and vanilla. Blend in cooled chocolate. Add egg yolks; mix well. Sift dry ingredients together and fold in sour cream; beat until smooth. Add coffee. Fold in egg whites. Pour into two 9-inch layer-cake pans lined on bottom with greased wax paper.

Bake in preheated 350° F. oven for about 30 minutes. Cool, and frost with Brown-Sugar Frosting.

Brown Sugar Frosting

1 cup granulated sugar

½ cup firmly packed brown sugar

3 tablespoons dark corn syrup

¼ cup water

2 egg whites

¼ teaspoon salt

¼ teaspoon cream of tartar

1 teaspoon vanilla extract

Put all ingredients except vanilla in top part of double boiler; mix well. Put over boiling water and beat until mixture will hold a peak, about 4 minutes. Remove from water; add vanilla.

Three-Egg Cake with Rum-Fudge Frosting

2⅓ cups flour

3 teaspoons baking powder

½ teaspoon salt

½ cup unsalted butter or margarine

1¼ cups sugar

3 eggs

1 cup milk

1 teaspoon vanilla extract

Rum-Fudge Frosting

In large bowl stir together flour, baking powder, and salt until well mixed; set aside. In large bowl of mixer cream butter and sugar until light. Beat in eggs until fluffy. Stir in flour mixture alternately with milk until well blended. Stir in vanilla. Turn into 2 greased and floured 9-inch round pans.

Bake in preheated 350° F. oven 20 to 30 minutes, or until pick inserted in center comes out clean. Cool in pan 10 minutes. Turn out on racks; cool. Fill and frost with Rum-Fudge Frosting.

Serves 12 to16.

Rum-Fudge Frosting

3 cups sugar

1 cup milk

4 squares (1 ounce each) unsweetened chocolate

3 tablespoons light corn syrup

⅓ cup unsalted butter or margarine

1 tablespoon dark rum or 1 teaspoon vanilla extract

In 3-quart saucepan over medium-high heat bring to boil sugar, milk, chocolate, and corn syrup, stirring often. Reduce heat to medium and cook, stirring occasionally, until syrup reaches soft-ball stage (234° F. on candy thermometer). Remove from heat. Add butter and rum but do not stir. Cool at room temperature (without stirring) to 110° F. or until bottom of pan feels just warm, about 1 hour.

Turn out into small bowl of mixer and beat at high speed until frosting is creamy and begins to hold its shape. If frosting becomes too stiff, add a few drops hot water; beat until creamy.

Note: Frosting will spread easily and maintain gloss if spatula is dipped in hot water.

Rum-Chocolate Cake

1 ounce (1 square) unsweetened chocolate
½ cup water
½ cup unsalted butter or margarine
1½ cups firmly packed light brown sugar
3 eggs
1¾ cups sifted cake flour
1½ teaspoons baking powder
¼ teaspoon salt
½ teaspoon baking soda
¼ cup dark rum
Rum-Chocolate Frosting

Melt chocolate in water over very low heat, stirring constantly. Cool.

In bowl of an electric mixer cream butter until fluffy. Gradually beat in sugar. Beat in eggs, one at a time, beating well after each addition. Sift flour with baking powder, salt, and soda. Add flour and chocolate alternately to egg mixture, beating until smooth. Stir in rum.

Line three 8-inch layer-cake pans or two 9-inch pans with greased wax paper. Distribute batter equally among pans. Bake 8-inch layers in moderate 350° F. oven 15 to 20 minutes, 9-inch layers 20 to 25 minutes, or until cake tests clean. Cool 5 minutes. Turn out on racks and peel off paper. When cool, fill and frost with Rum-Chocolate Frosting.

Rum-Chocolate Frosting

Melt 3 squares (1 ounce each) unsweetened chocolate with ½ cup dark rum over low heat. Stir in 1 teaspoon vanilla extract. Add 4 cups sifted confectioners' sugar, 1 cup at a time, beating well after each addition. Beat in ¼ cup softened unsalted butter. Add a little more rum if necessary for spreading consistency.

Chocolate-Apricot Trifle

Can be prepared a day ahead.

> ½ cup unsweetened cocoa
> ½ cup plus 2 tablespoons sugar, divided
> 2 teaspoons cornstarch
> ¼ teaspoon salt
> 2½ cups milk or half-and-half
> 1 egg, slightly beaten
> 1 teaspoon vanilla extract
> 1 cup apricot preserves (12 ounces)
> ¼ cup brandy or orange juice
> 1 cup heavy cream
> 1 angel-food cake, homemade or purchased, split in 4 layers
> ¼ cup slivered or sliced almonds, toasted

In small heavy saucepan mix cocoa, ½ cup sugar, cornstarch, and salt; stir in milk until blended. Stir over medium heat until mixture comes to boil and is smooth and thickened; remove from heat. Stir small amount into egg, then stir into chocolate sauce. Stir over very low heat 1 to 2 minutes or until slightly thickened (do not boil). Remove from heat; stir in vanilla. Cool, stirring occasionally; cover and chill.

Mix preserves and brandy until well blended. In small deep bowl beat cream and remaining 2 tablespoons sugar until stiff. Place 1 layer of cake in shallow bowl with flat bottom. Spread with apricot mixture, then whipped cream. Repeat with 2 more cake layers; top with fourth layer. Chill at least 2 hours or overnight.

Drizzle some sauce on cake; pour remainder around cake. Sprinkle with almonds.

Makes 8 servings.

Devil's Food Cake with Chocolate Shadow Icing

A delicious cake that can be made with any of three liquids—buttermilk for a fine texture and mild chocolate flavor, milk for a coarser texture and richer flavor, water for a fine texture and deep flavor.

   2 cups flour
   ⅓ cup cocoa
   1 teaspoon baking powder
   1 teaspoon baking soda
   ½ teaspoon salt
   ½ cup unsalted butter or margarine
   2 cups sugar
   2 eggs
   1½ cups buttermilk, milk, or water
   1 teaspoon vanilla extract
   Seven-Minute Frosting
   Chocolate Shadow Icing

In medium bowl stir flour, cocoa, baking powder, soda, and salt until well mixed; set aside.

In large bowl of mixer cream butter and sugar until light. Beat in eggs until light and fluffy. Stir in flour mixture alternately with buttermilk until well blended. Stir in vanilla. Turn into 2 greased 9-inch round pans lined with wax paper.

Bake in preheated 350° F. oven 25 to 35 minutes, or until pick inserted in center comes out clean. Cool in pans on racks 10 minutes. Turn out on racks; cool completely.

Fill and frost with Seven-Minute Frosting. Drizzle with Chocolate Shadow Icing. Let chocolate set before cutting.

Makes 12 to 16 servings.

Seven-Minute Frosting

1½ cups sugar

⅓ cup water

2 egg whites

1 teaspoon light corn syrup

½ teaspoon salt

1½ teaspoons vanilla extract

In top of double boiler mix sugar, water, egg whites, corn syrup, and salt. With mixer at high speed beat over simmering water about 7 minutes, or until frosting stands in stiff, glossy peaks. Remove from heat. Beat in vanilla.

Chocolate Shadow Icing

In small saucepan melt 2 squares (1 ounce each) semisweet chocolate. Stir in 3 tablespoons hot water until smooth. Mixture should be thin. If necessary, add more hot water.

Almond-Mocha Cake

8 eggs, separated

¾ cup sugar

½ teaspoon almond extract

¾ cup ground blanched almonds

½ cup flour

⅓ cup unsalted butter or margarine, melted and cooled

Mocha Buttercream

Toasted slivered or sliced almonds

Chocolate Curls (page 8)

In large bowl of mixer beat egg whites at medium speed until soft peaks form. Increase to high speed and gradually beat in sugar until stiff peaks form; set aside.

Stir almond extract into egg yolks to break up and blend. Fold about one-quarter of egg-white mixture into yolks; pour over remaining egg-white mixture. Sprinkle with almonds and flour, a few tablespoons at a time, folding in gently but thoroughly after each addition. Fold in only clear part of melted butter, discarding milky residue. Divide batter evenly among 3 greased paper-lined 8-inch layer pans.

Bake on center rack in preheated 350° F. oven 20 to 25 minutes, or until tops are golden and pick inserted in center comes out clean. Run small spatula around edge of layers, invert on racks and peel off paper, cool.

Reserving ½ cup Mocha Buttercream for decoration, spread about ¾ cup between layers, stacking. Frost top and sides of cake with remaining Buttercream. Pipe or spoon small dollops of reserved ½ cup Buttercream around rim of cake. Garnish center with almonds and Chocolate Curls. Chill at least 2 hours or overnight. Bring to room temperature before serving.

Makes 8 to 10 servings.

Mocha Buttercream

⅓ cup water

3 tablespoons instant coffee

3 squares (1 ounce each) unsweetened chocolate

1½ cups unsalted butter or margarine, softened

2½ cups confectioners' sugar

3 egg yolks

1 teaspoon vanilla extract

In small heavy saucepan over very low heat stir gently water, coffee, and chocolate until melted and smooth. Cool.

In small bowl of mixer cream butter, sugar, and egg yolks until smooth and well blended. Gradually add chocolate mixture; beat just until well blended. Stir in vanilla.

Makes enough to fill and frost three 8-inch layers.

Chocolate "Icebox" Cake

24 ladyfingers, split
8 ounces sweet cooking chocolate
¼ cup water
¼ cup sugar
4 eggs, separated
1 teaspoon vanilla extract
1 cup heavy cream, whipped
Chocolate Glaze (optional)

Line bottom and sides of 9 x 5 x 3-inch loaf pan with wax paper, letting paper extend above rim. Then line bottom and sides with ladyfingers, rounded sides against pan and as close together as possible. Set aside.

In heavy saucepan stir chocolate and water over low heat until chocolate is melted and smooth; remove from heat. Stir in sugar and well-beaten egg yolks; stir constantly over low heat until thick, smooth, and shiny, 3 to 5 minutes. Stir in vanilla; cool.

In large bowl of mixer beat egg whites until stiff. Fold chocolate mixture into egg whites until well blended, then fold in whipped cream.

Layer filling and remaining ladyfingers in ladyfingers-lined pan, starting and ending with filling. (If any filling remains, pour into dessert dish; chill and serve separately.) Chill cake 24 hours or until firm.

To remove cake from pan, firmly grasp extended paper and lift cake out. Peel paper away from sides. Carefully insert 2 wide spatulas between paper and bottom of cake and lift cake to serving platter. Drizzle with Chocolate Glaze.

Makes 8 to 10 servings.

Note: If desired, substitute "fingers" cut from sponge cake for ladyfingers.

Chocolate Glaze

In small heavy saucepan stir 2 squares (2 ounces) semisweet chocolate and 3 tablespoons water over low heat until melted and smooth; cool.

Potato-Chocolate Cake

⅔ cup unsalted butter or margarine, softened

2 cups sugar

4 eggs

1 cup hot mashed potatoes

2 squares (1 ounce each) unsweetened chocolate, melted

2 cups sifted flour

3½ teaspoons baking powder

1 teaspoon cinnamon

½ teaspoon nutmeg

½ teaspoon ground cloves

½ teaspoon mace

½ cup milk

1 cup chopped nuts

Chocolate Frosting

Cream butter and sugar until light and fluffy. Add eggs one at a time, beating thoroughly after each. Add potatoes and chocolate and mix well. Stir dry ingredients together and add alternately with milk, beating after each addition until smooth. Stir in nuts. Pour into greased and floured 13 x 9 x 2-inch pan.

Bake in preheated 350° F. oven 35 minutes, or until pick inserted in center comes out clean. Cool in pan on cake rack. Spread with Chocolate Frosting.

Chocolate Frosting

3 squares (1 ounce each) unsweetened chocolate

2 tablespoons unsalted butter or margarine

4½ cups sifted confectioners' sugar (about 1 pound)

¾ cup sour cream

¼ teaspoon salt

1 teaspoon vanilla extract

Melt chocolate and butter. Remove from heat and cool. Mix sugar, sour cream, and salt. Gradually add chocolate mixture and vanilla and beat well. If too soft to spread, chill until of desired consistency.

Rocky-Road Fudge Cake

1¾ cups flour

1½ cups sugar

¾ teaspoon salt

¾ teaspoon baking powder

½ teaspoon baking soda

¾ cup water

½ cup unsalted butter or margarine

3 squares (1 ounce each) unsweetened chocolate

2 eggs

⅓ cup buttermilk

1 teaspoon vanilla extract

12 to 16 marshmallows, halved

Chocolate-Nut Frosting

In large bowl stir together flour, sugar, salt, baking powder, and soda; set aside.

In small saucepan heat water, butter, and chocolate until butter and chocolate melt, stirring often; set aside.

In small bowl beat eggs, buttermilk, and vanilla with fork until blended. Stir egg mixture and chocolate mixture into flour mixture just until blended. Pour into greased and floured 9 x 9 x 2-inch pan.

Bake in preheated 350° F. oven 20 to 30 minutes, or until pick inserted in center comes out clean. Cool in pan on rack 10 minutes. Turn out on rack. Arrange marshmallows cut side down on warm cake. Cool completely. Frost with Chocolate-Nut Frosting, filling spaces between marshmallows.

Makes 12 to 16 servings.

Chocolate-Nut Frosting

4 squares (1 ounce each) unsweetened chocolate

2 cups confectioners' sugar, divided

3 tablespoons water

4 egg yolks

6 tablespoons unsalted butter or margarine, softened

½ cup finely chopped nuts

In medium saucepan melt chocolate. Remove from heat. Beat in 1 cup sugar and water until smooth. Add remaining 1 cup sugar and egg yolks, beating until smooth. Beat in butter and nuts.

Chocolate Pound Cake

2 cups flour

1 teaspoon baking soda

½ cup unsalted butter or margarine, softened

1½ cups packed brown sugar

2 eggs

1 cup sour cream, at room temperature

1 teaspoon vanilla extract

2 squares (1 ounce each) unsweetened chocolate,
    melted and cooled

Mix flour and baking soda; set aside.

In large bowl cream butter until fluffy; add brown sugar; beat until blended. Add eggs, one at a time, beating thoroughly after each. Gradually beat in flour mixture just until blended and smooth. Beat in sour cream and vanilla until blended. Beat in chocolate until well blended. Pour into greased 9 x 5 x 3-inch loaf pan.

Bake in preheated 325° F. oven 60 to 70 minutes, or until top springs back when pressed lightly with finger. Cool on rack in pan 10 minutes; carefully remove from pan; cool completely on rack.

Makes eighteen ½-inch-thick slices.

Marble Cake

3 cups flour

4 teaspoons baking powder

¾ teaspoon salt

1 cup unsalted butter or margarine

2 cups granulated sugar

4 eggs

1 cup milk

1 teaspoon vanilla extract

2 squares (1 ounce each) unsweetened chocolate, melted

3 tablespoons hot water

¼ teaspoon almond extract

⅛ teaspoon baking soda

Chocolate Glaze or confectioners' sugar (optional)

Stir together flour, baking powder, and salt; set aside.

In large bowl or mixer cream butter and granulated sugar until light. Beat in eggs until very light and fluffy. Stir in flour mixture alternating with milk, blending lightly but thoroughly. Stir in vanilla. Transfer half the batter to small bowl and stir in chocolate, water, almond extract, and soda until well blended. Alternate spoonfuls of each batter in greased 10-inch fluted tube pan. With spatula, gently swirl batters together to marbleize.

Bake in preheated 350° F. oven 50 minutes, or until pick inserted half-way between tube and edge of cake comes out clean. Cool in pan on rack 10 minutes. Turn out on rack; cool completely. Drizzle with Chocolate Glaze or sprinkle with confectioners' sugar

Makes 16 to 20 servings.

Chocolate Glaze

In small heavy saucepan over low heat melt 3 squares (1 ounce each) semisweet chocolate. Stir in 4 tablespoons hot water or enough to make thin glaze.

Chocolate Cream Roll

Make early in day or day ahead.

   ¼ cup cocoa
   2 tablespoons flour
   6 eggs
   1¼ cups confectioners' sugar
   1½ teaspoons vanilla extract
   About ¼ cup granulated sugar
   Cream Filling
   Thin Chocolate Glaze
   Whipped cream (optional)
   Chopped pistachio nuts (optional)

Grease 15 x 10 x 1-inch jelly-roll pan, then line with wax paper, extending paper at short ends. Grease paper; set pan aside.
   Stir together cocoa and flour until well blended; set aside.
   In large bowl of mixer beat eggs at high speed until very light, about 5 minutes. Gradually beat in confectioners' sugar, and beat until very fluffy and lemon-colored, about 5 minutes. Fold cocoa mixture and vanilla into egg mixture until well blended. Pour batter into prepared pan and spread evenly.
   Bake in preheated 350° F. oven 20 minutes, or until pick inserted in center comes out clean. Cool in pan on rack 5 minutes.
   Loosen edges of cake with thin-bladed spatula. Sprinkle clean dish towel generously with granulated sugar and invert cake onto towel. Peel off paper. Starting at short end, roll up cake and towel as for jelly roll. Cool on rack.
   Unroll. Spread cake with Cream Filling. Reroll *without towel*. Place on platter. Frost with Thin Chocolate Glaze. Chill several hours or overnight. Garnish with dollops of whipped cream and pistachios.
   Makes 10 to 12 servings.

Cream Filling

In small bowl of mixer whip 1 cup heavy cream and 2 tablespoons confectioners' sugar until soft peaks form (do not overwhip).

Thin Chocolate Glaze
In small saucepan melt 5 squares (1 ounce each) semisweet chocolate. Stir in ⅓ cup hot water until smooth. Spread over roll.

French Chocolate Roll

If you wish, serve half and freeze the rest.

6 squares (1 ounce each) semisweet chocolate

2 tablespoons strong coffee

1 teaspoon vanilla extract

6 eggs, separated

⅛ teaspoon salt

¾ cup granulated sugar

3 tablespoons unsweetened cocoa, divided

3 tablespoons confectioners' sugar, divided

1 cup heavy cream

Garnish (optional; see Note)

Grease 15 x 10 x 1-inch jelly-roll pan. Line with wax paper, extending it a few inches at narrow ends; set aside.

In top of double boiler over hot (not boiling) water, or in heavy saucepan over very low heat, melt chocolate in coffee. Remove from heat; stir in vanilla until smooth; set aside to cool.

In large bowl beat egg whites with salt until they hold soft peaks. Add granulated sugar 1 tablespoon at a time, beating well after each until mixture forms stiff, shining peaks; set aside.

Stir egg yolks to break up. Stir in chocolate mixture until well blended. Fold one-quarter of egg-white mixture into chocolate mixture until well blended. Add remaining whites; fold gently until blended. Pour into prepared pan; spread evenly.

Bake on middle rack in preheated 350° F. oven 16 to 18 minutes, or until top is firm. Remove from oven; cool in pan on rack.

Run small knife around edges to loosen pastry. Sift 2 tablespoons each unsweetened cocoa and confectioners' sugar onto clean kitchen towel over a 15 x 10-inch area. Invert pan onto coated towel. Working quickly, remove pan and peel off paper; cool cake completely.

Meanwhile, beat cream with remaining cocoa and confectioners' sugar until stiff. Spread over pastry to within ½ inch of edges. Lift one long side of towel until pastry rolls inward; continue until you have a roll. (Roll will have cracks.) Trim off ends; transfer roll, seam side down, onto sheet of foil. Wrap foil firmly around roll; chill several hours or overnight.

Remove foil; transfer roll to long board or platter. With sharp knife, cut in 1-inch slices.

Makes 14 slices.

Note: For garnish, beat ½ cup heavy cream with 1½ teaspoons each unsweetened cocoa and confectioners' sugar until stiff. Spoon small dollops on roll; sprinkle with Chocolate Shavings (page 8).

Chilled Chocolate-Orange Loaf

½ cup unsalted butter or margarine, softened

½ cup confectioners' sugar, plus additional for top

1 teaspoon grated orange peel

1 tablespoon orange juice

4 squares (1 ounce each) semisweet chocolate, or ⅔ cup semisweet chocolate pieces, melted and cooled

1 egg

1 package (3 ounces) ladyfingers, separated in 4 rows

Chocolate Shadow for garnish (optional)

In small bowl beat butter and sugar until light-colored and creamy. Beat in orange peel, juice, and chocolate until well blended.

Line bottom and sides of 7 x 4-inch loaf pan with plastic wrap. Place a row of ladyfingers, rounded sides down, on bottom; spread with one-quarter of chocolate mixture. Continue to layer ladyfingers and chocolate mixture, ending with chocolate mixture. Cover with plastic wrap; chill several hours or overnight.

Unmold onto platter; peel off plastic wrap. Dust top lightly with confectioners' sugar; drizzle with Chocolate Shadow. Refrigerate until ready to serve. Slice crosswise with serrated knife.

Makes 8 servings.

Chocolate Shadow

In small heavy saucepan over low heat, stir 1 square (1 ounce) chopped semisweet chocolate in 2 tablespoons water until smooth. Cool.

Chocolate-Raspberry Cupcakes

A chocolate and brown-sugar version of a Swiss cupcake.

> 2 squares (1 ounce each) unsweetened chocolate
> 1 cup milk
> ½ cup unsalted butter or margarine, softened
> 1 teaspoon vanilla extract
> 1 cup packed light brown sugar
> 1¾ cups all-purpose flour
> 1 teaspoon baking soda
> ½ teaspoon salt
> 3 eggs, beaten
> Seedless raspberry jam
> Sweetened whipped cream
> Toasted coconut

Combine chocolate and ½ cup milk in small heavy saucepan. Melt, stirring over low heat; cool. Cream butter and vanilla. Gradually add sugar and cream until light and fluffy. Mix well flour, soda, and salt. Add to creamed mixture alternately with remaining milk, blending until smooth. Blend in eggs and chocolate mixture. Fill 2½-inch paper-lined foil baking cups about two-thirds full.

Bake in preheated 350° F. oven 25 minutes, or until done. Cool on rack.

Remove cakes from paper cups and split each in two layers. Spread bottom layer with desired amount of raspberry jam. Replace tops and add a heaping tablespoon of whipped cream. Sprinkle with coconut.

Makes about 2 dozen.

Note: If desired, substitute Basic Hot-Fudge Sauce (page 145) for the whipped cream.

Surprise Chocolate Cupcakes

2 squares (1 ounce each) unsweetened chocolate
1 cup milk
½ cup unsalted butter
1½ cups sugar
2 cups sifted all-purpose flour
1 teaspoon baking soda
½ teaspoon salt
3 eggs, beaten
1 teaspoon vanilla extract
1 teaspoon lemon flavoring
The Surprise

Melt chocolate with ½ cup milk over low heat; cool.

Cream butter and sugar together. Sift flour with baking soda and salt; add to butter mixture alternately with remaining ½ cup milk. Add beaten eggs. Add chocolate to batter and stir in flavorings. Pour into greased 2½-inch muffin pans, filling cups about two-thirds full.

Bake in preheated 350° F. oven for 25 minutes, or until cupcakes test done. Cool and prepare Surprise.

Makes about 24.

The Surprise

Cut tops off cupcakes and reserve. Scoop out interior carefully so that cake shells don't break. Fill with sugared fresh raspberries or well-drained thawed, frozen raspberries. Top with sweetened whipped cream. Place cake tops on whipped cream at an angle and decorate each with a raspberry or a candied cherry.

Chocolate-Pecan Torte

1½ cups (9 ounces) semisweet chocolate pieces

½ cup unsalted butter, softened

½ cup sugar

4 egg yolks

4 egg whites, stiffly beaten

1 cup pecans, chopped in blender or minced

¼ cup all-purpose flour

½ cup apricot preserves

Whipped cream (optional)

Melt 1 cup chocolate in top of double boiler over hot water. Cool.

Cream butter and sugar until light. Add egg yolks one at a time, beating thoroughly after each. Blend in chocolate. Fold egg whites into batter with nuts and flour. Blend well. Pour into 9-inch layer pan lined on bottom with paper.

Bake in 350° F. oven about 25 minutes. Turn out on cake rack. Spread top and sides with apricot preserves while cake is still warm. Melt remaining chocolate and spread thin layer on top of preserves.

Cool cake, cut in thin wedges, and serve, with whipped cream if desired.

Black-Bread and Chocolate Torte

2 cups fine fresh pumpernickel crumbs, made in blender
    from firm-type bread

⅓ cup light rum

6 eggs, separated

⅛ teaspoon salt

1 cup sugar

1 teaspoon vanilla extract

4 squares (1 ounce each) semisweet chocolate, finely
    grated in blender

⅓ cup walnuts, finely grated in blender

Rum-Flavored Whipped Cream

Chocolate Curls (page 8)

Grease bottoms of three 8-inch layer-cake pans. Line with wax-paper circles cut to fit. Grease paper and set aside.

Put crumbs in mixing bowl, sprinkle with rum, and set aside.

In large bowl of electric mixer beat egg whites with salt at medium speed until soft peaks form. Increase speed to high and gradually beat in sugar, beating until stiff peaks form. Stir vanilla into egg yolks to break up and blend. Fold about one-quarter of egg-white mixture into yolks, then pour this mixture over remaining egg-white mixture. Sprinkle with bread crumbs, chocolate, and walnuts, a few tablespoons at a time, folding in gently but thoroughly after each addition. Divide batter evenly among pans and bake on rack in center of preheated 350° F. oven 30 minutes, or until pick inserted in center comes out clean. Cool completely in pans on cake racks.

Run a small spatula around edges, invert on racks, and peel off papers. To assemble torte, sandwich layers with about one-third of the Rum-Flavored Whipped Cream. Frost with remaining cream, piping some through pastry bag with fluted tip to decorate rim. Decorate center with Chocolate Curls. Chill at least 1 hour before serving.

Makes 10 servings.

Rum-Flavored Whipped Cream

Beat 2 cups heavy cream until soft peaks form. Gradually beat in 3 tablespoons sugar until stiff. Fold in 2 tablespoons light rum.

Sacher Torte

The world-famous chocolate torte from the Hotel Sacher in Vienna. Make cake 24 hours before frosting.

> ¾ cup unsalted butter or margarine, softened
>
> ¾ cup sugar
>
> 6½ squares (1 ounce each) semisweet chocolate, melted and cooled
>
> 8 eggs, separated
>
> 1 cup cake flour, stirred and lightly spooned into measuring cup
>
> 2 egg whites
>
> 2 tablespoons apricot jam or preserves, slightly heated
>
> Chocolate Fondant Frosting
>
> Whipped-cream rosettes (optional)

Grease 9-inch springform pan well and set aside.

In large bowl of electric mixer cream butter; gradually beat in sugar until light and fluffy. Beat in chocolate, then egg yolks, about 2 at a time, until well blended. Stir in flour. Beat the 10 egg whites until stiff but not dry; add about one-third to chocolate mixture and blend well. Fold in remaining egg whites gently but thoroughly. Pour into prepared pan.

Bake on rack in center of preheated 275° F. oven about 1 hour 15 minutes, or until torte pulls away from sides of pan and pick inserted in center comes out clean. Cool in pan on cake rack 10 minutes. Run small spatula around edge, remove ring, and cool thoroughly. Cover loosely with wax paper and let stand 24 hours.

To assemble, remove torte from cake-pan bottom and put on serving platter. (Top may be slightly soggy so cut off in thin layer, if desired.) Spread top with jam. Pour Chocolate Fondant Frosting on center of cake and with small spatula quickly spread over top and sides of cake. Decorate top with large whipped-cream rosettes piped through pastry bag with fluted tip, or top each wedge with a dollop of whipped cream.

Makes 12 servings.

Chocolate Fondant Frosting

Melt 7 squares (1 ounce each) semisweet chocolate in top of double boiler over hot water. Combine 1 cup sugar and ⅓ cup water in small saucepan and bring to boil over medium heat (do not stir). Cook 3 to 5 minutes, just until thin syrup forms and a drop placed between thumb and index finger feels sticky (be careful not to burn fingers), or until candy thermometer reads 220° F. Gradually add syrup to chocolate and stir until well blended and frosting coats spoon but is still glossy.

Note: Do not overcook syrup, or frosting will be dull and sugary.

Mocha Cream Torte

1 package (6 ounces) semisweet chocolate pieces

⅓ cup water

1 teaspoon baking soda

4 eggs, separated

1 teaspoon vanilla extract

¼ teaspoon salt

½ cup flour

½ cup sugar

Coffee Topping

Put chocolate and water in heavy saucepan and heat slowly, stirring, until chocolate is melted and mixture is smooth. Remove from heat and stir in soda. Beat in egg yolks, vanilla, and salt, then blend in flour. Beat egg whites until soft peaks are formed. Gradually add sugar and beat until stiff. Fold carefully but thoroughly into first mixture. Put in 3 greased 8-inch layer-cake pans lined on bottom with wax paper.

Bake in preheated 375° F. oven about 15 minutes. Loosen around edges and turn out on cake racks. Peel off paper, cool thoroughly, fill and frost with topping. Chill until ready to serve.

Makes 10 to12 servings.

Note: This is a sponge-type cake; layers will not be thick.

Coffee Topping

Combine and beat with rotary or electric mixer until very thick 1½ cups heavy cream, ¾ cup packed light brown sugar, ½ teaspoon instant coffee, and ⅛ teaspoon almond extract.

Chocolate Cheesecake

Chocolate-Wafer Crust
3 packages (8 ounces each) cream cheese, softened
¾ cup sugar
3 eggs
8 squares (1 ounce each) semisweet chocolate, melted
½ cup strong black coffee, cooled
½ cup sour cream
1 teaspoon vanilla extract
⅛ teaspoon salt
Unsweetened whipped cream and Chocolate Curls
    (page 8) (optional)

Prepare crust and chill.

Beat cheese in large bowl of electric mixer until light and fluffy. Gradually beat in sugar. Add eggs one at a time, beating well after each. Beat in chocolate, coffee, sour cream, vanilla, and salt until smooth. Pour into prepared pan.

Bake in preheated 350° F. oven 1 hour, or until firm in center. Cool on cake rack, then chill, if preferred. Run spatula around edge of cake to loosen, then remove sides of pan. Garnish with whipped cream and Chocolate Curls, if desired.

Makes 16 servings.

Chocolate-Wafer Crust

Mix together 1 cup finely crushed chocolate-wafer crumbs, 2 tablespoons sugar, and ¼ cup melted unsalted butter. Press on bottom of 9-inch springform or other loose-bottom pan.

Chocolate-Almond Cheesecake

An easy-to-prepare, luscious, creamy cheesecake. The almond flavor is more pronounced if cake chills overnight. Garnish just before serving.

  1 cup chocolate-wafer crumbs
  ¼ cup unsalted butter or margarine, melted
  2 packages (8 ounces each) cream cheese, at
      room temperature
  1 cup sugar
  ⅓ cup unsweetened cocoa
  2 eggs
  5 tablespoons almond-flavored liqueur, divided
  ½ cup sliced almonds
  1 cup heavy cream
  Candied violets for garnish (optional)

Mix crumbs and butter until well moistened; refrigerate in large bowl. Press onto bottom of greased 8-inch springform pan.

Beat cream cheese, sugar, and cocoa until blended; add eggs and 3 tablespoons liqueur. Beat just until smooth. Turn into prepared pan; sprinkle evenly with almonds.

Bake in preheated 375° F. oven 35 minutes (do not open oven door during baking), or until sides are firm and slightly raised (center will still be soft). Remove pan to rack. While still hot run a thin knife or spatula around edge of pan to loosen cake. Cool cake completely in pan before removing sides. Chill, covered, at least 4 hours before serving.

In small bowl combine heavy cream with remaining liqueur; chill 1 hour. Beat until stiff peaks form. Pipe or drop spoonfuls around sides and in center of cake. Garnish cream with some of the loose toasted almonds from cake and candied violets.

Makes 10 servings.

New York City Chocolate Cheesecake

This dense chocolate cheesecake can be refrigerated up to two days or frozen.

> 3 packages (8 ounces each) cream cheese, at
>   room temperature
> 1 teaspoon vanilla extract
> ⅛ teaspoon salt
> 1 cup sugar
> 12 squares (1 ounce each) semisweet chocolate, or 2 cups
>   chocolate pieces, melted and cooled
> 3 eggs
> 1 cup sour cream
> Chocolate-Wafer Crust (page 43)
> Whipped cream (optional)

In large bowl beat cream cheese until very smooth. Add vanilla, salt, and sugar; beat until very smooth. Add chocolate; beat until well blended. Add eggs one at a time, scraping bowl and beating well after each. Add sour cream; beat until smooth. Spoon into crumb crust; smooth top.

Bake 1 hour in lower third of preheated 375° F. oven. (Cake will still be soft.) Cool completely on rack. Leave in pan; cover top with foil; refrigerate overnight.

With sharp, heavy knife cut around sides of crust, pressing knife blade firmly against pan as you cut. Press gently under crust; ease around to release cake completely from bottom of pan. Cake will be firm and easy to transfer. (At this point cake can be refrigerated or wrapped airtight and frozen. If frozen, thaw, wrapped, in refrigerator overnight.)

Place on large flat platter. Serve cold with whipped cream or pipe border around edge.

Makes 16 servings.

An Assortment
of Pies

Apple pie might be America's favorite, but true chocolate lovers know that it doesn't compare with the rich, deep goodness of a fluffy Chocolate Cream Pie or the special contrasting tastes of a Rum-Chocolate-Pecan Pie. Here is a selection of the best chocolate pies you'll ever taste, all filled with dark chocolate, clouds of creamy topping, and scrumptious crusts. Easy to prepare, these pies are perfect for any occasion, or for simply enjoying all by yourself. Try the Chocolate Chiffon Pie, a light lovely dessert that's absolutely yummy! And if you're planning a special affair, the Fudge Walnut Pie à la Mode with Hot-Fudge Sauce is irresistible. And who said meringue pies only come in lemon? Here's a recipe for Chocolate Meringue Pie that will titillate any palate, a coup in chocolate circles. And not to be outdone by the cheesecake coterie, Chocolate Cheese Pie is a delicious treat, perfect for sneaking as a midnight snack.

Chocolate Chiffon Pie

1 envelope unflavored gelatin

¾ cup sugar, divided

¼ teaspoon salt

1 cup milk

2 squares (1 ounce each) unsweetened chocolate

4 eggs, separated

1 teaspoon vanilla extract

Baked 9-inch pie shell

Sweetened whipped cream

Chocolate syrup (optional)

In top part of small double boiler, mix gelatin, 2 tablespoons sugar, and salt. Add milk and chocolate and put over simmering water. Stir until chocolate melts, then beat with rotary beater until blended. Beat egg yolks and 2 tablespoons sugar together. Stir in small amount of hot mixture, then stir back into double boiler. Cook, stirring, until thickened. Cool, stirring occasionally, then add vanilla.

Beat egg whites until foamy. Gradually add ½ cup sugar, beating until stiff but not dry. Fold into gelatin mixture and pile lightly in pie shell. Chill until firm. Top with whipped cream, and drizzle with chocolate syrup, if desired.

Chocolate Cheese Pie

Butter Crust

1½ cups creamed cottage cheese

1 package (3 ounces) cream cheese

3 eggs

¾ cup sugar

2 squares (1 ounce each) semisweet chocolate, grated

¾ cup sour cream

Chocolate Curls (optional) (page 8)

Prepare crust and, while baking, prepare filling. Beat cheeses together in electric mixer until fairly smooth. Add eggs one at a time, beating well after each. Add sugar and beat until blended. Sprinkle half the chocolate in crust and pour in half the cheese mixture. Repeat.

Bake in preheated 325° F. oven 1 hour, or until knife inserted near center comes out clean. Put pie on wire rack and spread with sour cream. Cool completely, then sprinkle with Chocolate Curls, if desired. Store any remaining pie in refrigerator.

Butter Crust

Beat in electric mixer until smooth ½ cup softened unsalted butter or margarine, 1 cup flour, and 2 tablespoons confectioners' sugar. Press evenly on bottom and sides of 9-inch pie pan. With fork, press edge of crust to edge of pan. Prick bottom of crust.

Bake in preheated 400 F.° oven about 10 minutes.

Chocolate Cream Pie

Delicious with Meringue or Whipped-Cream Topping—take your pick! Prepare pie at least 4 hours before serving, but do not prepare a day ahead.

Chocolate-Walnut Pie Shell or 9-inch baked pie shell
1¼ cups sugar
⅓ cup cornstarch
¼ teaspoon salt
3 cups milk
3 squares (1 ounce each) unsweetened chocolate
4 egg yolks, slightly beaten
1 teaspoon vanilla extract
Meringue Topping or Whipped-Cream Topping, as preferred

Prepare pie shell; set aside.

In large heavy saucepan mix sugar, cornstarch, and salt. Gradually stir in milk until smooth. Add chocolate. Stir over medium to medium-low heat until mixture thickens and comes to boil. Gradually blend a little chocolate mixture into egg yolks; add to remaining chocolate mixture.

Stir over very low heat 2 to 3 minutes longer, or until slightly thicker. Remove from heat; stir in vanilla. Pour into pie shell.

Meringue Topping

In small bowl or mixer beat until foamy 4 egg whites at room temperature, ¼ teaspoon cream of tartar, and dash of salt. Beat in ½ cup sugar, 1 tablespoon at a time, until stiff and glossy. Beat in ½ teaspoon vanilla extract.

Immediately heap Meringue on hot filling, and spread carefully to seal edge of shell. Bake in preheated 425° F. oven 3 to 5 minutes, or until Meringue is lightly browned. Cool slightly, then chill at least 2 hours. If desired, garnish with Chocolate-Walnut Pie-Shell crumbs or shredded chocolate.

Whipped-Cream Topping

Place plastic wrap right on filling. Chill pie at least 2 hours. About 1 to 2 hours before serving, remove plastic wrap and spread pie attractively with whipped cream.

Makes 8 to 10 servings.

Chocolate-Walnut Pie Shell

    1 cup flour
    ¼ cup finely chopped walnuts
    1 square (1 ounce) unsweetened chocolate, grated coarse
    2 tablespoons sugar
    ⅛ teaspoon salt
    ⅓ cup shortening
    About 2 tablespoons cold water

In bowl mix flour, walnuts, chocolate, sugar, and salt. Cut in shortening until mixture resembles coarse crumbs. Sprinkle with water, about 1 tablespoon at a time, mixing just until ball forms.

On lightly floured surface roll out pastry to large circle. Fit into 9-inch pie plate; trim and flute edge. Prick bottom and sides with fork.

Bake in preheated 375° F. oven 20 to 25 minutes, or until lightly browned at edge. Cool.

If desired, roll out and bake any scraps of dough in ungreased pan 15 to 20 minutes or until lightly browned. Cool. Crumble coarse and use as garnish.

Black-Bottom Pie

1 envelope unflavored gelatin

1¾ cups milk

4 eggs, separated

1 cup granulated sugar

½ teaspoon salt

4 teaspoons cornstarch

2 squares (1 ounce each) unsweetened chocolate

1 teaspoon vanilla extract

Gingersnap-Crumb Crust

3 tablespoons rum

1 cup heavy cream, whipped

2 tablespoons confectioners' sugar

Soften gelatin in ¼ cup milk for 5 minutes.

Scald remaining 1½ cups milk in top part of double boiler over boiling water. Beat egg yolks. Blend in ½ cup granulated sugar, salt, and cornstarch. Add milk slowly, stirring constantly. Return to double boiler and cook over simmering water, stirring constantly, for 4 minutes, or until custard coats spoon.

Remove from heat. Reserve ½ cup custard. Add gelatin to remainder of hot custard and stir until dissolved; chill.

Melt 1½ ounces chocolate; stir in reserved ½ cup custard and vanilla. Beat with rotary beater until blended; cool. Pour into Gingersnap-Crumb Crust; chill until firm.

When remaining custard begins to set, add rum. Beat egg whites until stiff but not dry. Gradually beat in remaining ½ cup granulated sugar. Fold into custard. Pour over chocolate mixture in pie. Chill until firm.

Combine whipped cream and confectioners' sugar. Put on pie with pastry tube or spread on top. Shave remaining ½ square (½ ounce) chocolate over cream. Chill before serving.

Makes 6 to 8 servings.

Gingersnap-Crumb Crust

Blend thoroughly 1¼ cups fine gingersnap crumbs and ¼ cup unsalted butter. Press onto bottom and sides of deep 9-inch pie pan, using back of spoon. Bake in preheated 350° F. oven about 10 minutes. Chill.

Dark-Chocolate Mousse Pie

4 tablespoons finely chopped pecans, divided

8 eggs, separated

⅛ teaspoon salt

1 to 2 tablespoons brandy

1 cup sugar

4 squares (1 ounce each) unsweetened chocolate,
    melted and cooled

½ cup heavy cream

Brandy Whipped Cream (optional)

Grease 9-inch pie plate well and sprinkle with 3 tablespoons pecans; set aside.

In large bowl of mixer beat egg whites at high speed until stiff but not dry; set aside.

In small bowl of mixer mix egg yolks, salt, and brandy. Add sugar gradually and beat at high speed until thick and light-colored. Add chocolate and beat until well blended. Stir one-quarter of egg whites into chocolate mixture, then pour chocolate mixture over remaining whites and fold in gently but thoroughly. Pour about half the mixture into prepared pie plate to ½ inch from rim. Bake in preheated 350° F. oven 18 to 20 minutes, or until still lightly moist when pick is inserted in center; cool on rack.

Meanwhile, whip cream just until soft peaks form; fold into remaining mousse and chill. Spoon onto cooled baked mousse and chill overnight.

Just before serving, decorate with dollops of Brandy Whipped Cream and sprinkle with remaining 1 tablespoon pecans.

Makes 8 to 10 servings.

Brandy Whipped Cream

In small bowl of mixer stir ½ cup heavy cream, 2 tablespoons sugar, and 1 tablespoon brandy; chill at least 1 hour. Whip until soft peaks form.

Chocolate Meringue Pie

Pie

    1 cup sugar

    ¼ cup cornstarch

    ¼ teaspoon salt

    4 tablespoons unsalted butter or margarine

    3 squares (1 ounce each) unsweetened chocolate

    1½ cups warm water

    3 eggs, beaten

    Grated peel of 1 lemon or orange, or 1 teaspoon vanilla extract

    8-inch baked pie crust (or substitute crust of crushed
        chocolate cookies, gingersnaps, or graham crackers)

Mix sugar, cornstarch, and salt; set aside.

    Melt butter in heavy 3-quart saucepan over low heat. Add chocolate and stir to melt; remove from heat. Stir in water and sugar mixture, then stir in eggs. Cook and stir over low heat about 15 minutes, or until slightly thickened and smooth. Stir in lemon peel. Cool, stirring occasionally. Pour into cooled pie crust and set aside.

Meringue

    4 egg whites

    ½ teaspoon cream of tartar

    6 tablespoons confectioners' sugar

    1 teaspoon vanilla extract

Beat egg whites until frothy. Add cream of tartar and continue beating until egg whites stand up in soft peaks. Beat in sugar 1 tablespoon at a time. Do not overbeat; egg whites should stand in peaks, but should not be stiff. Add vanilla. Spread in decorative design over chocolate pie filling.

    Bake 10 to 15 minutes in preheated 350° F. oven, until peaks are slightly browned. Cool pie and then refrigerate. Filling will become firm as pie chills.

    Makes 8 to 10 servings.

Easy Chocolate Ice-Cream Pie

1½ cups coconut-macaroon crumbs (about ten
   1½-inch macaroons)

¼ cup light rum

1 quart chocolate ice cream, slightly softened

1 square (1 ounce) semisweet chocolate, chopped coarse

2 tablespoons water

¼ cup toasted shredded coconut (optional)

Place crumbs in 9-inch pie plate; sprinkle with rum. When rum is absorbed (about 5 minutes), press crumbs onto bottom and up sides of pie plate. Spoon ice cream into shell; freeze if too soft.

In small, heavy saucepan over lower heat, stir chocolate and water until smooth. Cool. Drizzle over ice cream; place in freezer until firm. Sprinkle with coconut before serving.

Makes 8 servings.

Rum-Chocolate-Pecan Pie

½ cup unsalted butter or margarine, softened

2 egg yolks

2 cups confectioners' sugar

¼ teaspoon salt

¼ cup dark rum

1 teaspoon lemon juice

2 squares (1 ounce each) unsweetened chocolate,
   melted and cooled

2 cups pecan halves, coarsely broken

1 cup heavy cream, whipped

9-inch pie shell, baked and cooled

Rum Whipped Cream (optional)

In large bowl of mixer combine butter, egg yolks, sugar, salt, rum, and lemon juice. Blend at low speed, then beat at high speed until smooth and fluffy. With rubber spatula stir in chocolate until well blended. Fold in pecans, then whipped cream. Pile filling into pie shell and chill overnight.

Remove from refrigerator 1 hour before serving. With pastry tube pipe Rum Whipped Cream on pie to make a decorative topping, or garnish with cream around edge.

Makes 12 servings.

Rum Whipped Cream

In small bowl of mixer stir 1 cup heavy cream, 2 tablespoons sugar, and 1 to 2 teaspoons dark rum; chill at least 1 hour. Whip until stiff.

Fudge Walnut Pie à la Mode with Hot-Fudge Sauce

1 cup sugar

½ cup unsalted butter or margarine, softened

2 eggs

2 tablespoons milk

1 teaspoon vanilla extract

⅓ cup flour mixed with ⅛ teaspoon salt

2 squares (1 ounce each) unsweetened chocolate,
   broken in pieces

Walnuts, broken in pieces

Vanilla ice cream

Hot-Fudge Sauce

In small bowl of mixer blend together sugar, butter, and eggs. Beat at high speed until very fluffy, about 5 minutes. Using low speed, blend in milk, vanilla, and flour mixture, then blend in chocolate. Stir in ½ cup walnuts. Spread in greased 9-inch pie plate.

Bake in preheated 350° F. oven 35 minutes, or until puffed in center and pick inserted in center barely comes out clean. (Pie will rise during baking, then sink slightly while cooling.) Cool completely on rack.

Cut in wedges; top each wedge with a scoop of vanilla ice cream and some Hot-Fudge Sauce. Sprinkle with walnuts.

Makes 8 to 10 servings.

Hot-Fudge Sauce

In saucepan melt ⅓ cup unsalted butter or margarine and 2 squares (1 ounce each) unsweetened chocolate. Blend in 1 cup sugar, 1 cup heavy cream, and ⅛ teaspoon salt. Stir over low heat until hot, about 5 minutes. Remove from heat; stir in 2 teaspoons vanilla extract.

Makes about 2 cups.

Note: Store any leftover sauce, covered, in refrigerator. Reheat over very low heat, adding a little hot water if necessary.

All Kinds of Cookies

What could be more satisfying than whipping up a batch of crispy, golden chocolate-chip cookies for filling lunch pails and hungry bellies? Included are easy-to-make drop cookies, refrigerator cookies, macaroons, shortbreads, and more. They are perfect as gifts, wrapped in shiny paper or nestled in a decorative tin. And they travel very well through the mail or in your luggage if you keep these tips in mind:

- Pack cookies in single layers with wax paper between each. This is also a good idea for candies.
- Pack cookies tight in rigid containers such as cookie tins, coffee cans, oatmeal cylinders, or boxes.
- Make sure all containers, especially jars, are well cushioned. Gift-wrap, then put in slightly larger box, filling spaces between with shredded or crumpled paper, foil, plastic wrap, or popcorn.
- Wrap for shipping and mark "Fragile."

Chocolate-Chip Oatmeal Cookies

¾ cup packed brown sugar

½ cup unsalted butter or margarine, softened

1 egg

1¼ cups quick-cooking rolled oats

¾ cup flour

½ cup (3 ounces) semisweet chocolate chips

¾ teaspoon baking soda

In large bowl of electric mixer cream brown sugar and butter until light and fluffy. Beat in egg. Stir in oats, flour, chips, and soda. Drop by heaping teaspoonfuls 1 inch apart on greased cookie sheets.

Bake in preheated 375° F. oven 12 minutes, or until lightly browned. Cool on wire racks. Store in tightly covered container.

Makes about 48.

Chocolate-Oatmeal Crunchies

1½ cups sifted all-purpose flour

1 teaspoon salt

¾ teaspoon baking soda

¾ cup shortening

¾ cup granulated sugar

¾ cup packed brown sugar

2 eggs

1 teaspoon vanilla extract

2 cups quick-cooking or regular rolled oats (not instant)

1 package (6 ounces) semisweet chocolate pieces

1 package (4 ounces) shredded coconut

Sift first 3 ingredients together. Cream shortening and sugars until light. Add eggs and vanilla and beat well. Stir in sifted dry ingredients. Add remaining ingredients and mix well. Drop by rounded tablespoonfuls 2 inches apart on ungreased cookie sheets.

Bake in 350° F. oven 18 to 20 minutes. Remove from sheets and cool on cake racks.

Makes about 5 dozen.

Note: Coconut can be omitted, if preferred. Decrease baking time slightly.

Mocha Drop Cookies

¼ cup unsalted butter, softened

1 cup confectioners' sugar

1 egg

3 tablespoons strong coffee

2 squares (1 ounce each) semisweet chocolate,
    melted and cooled

1¾ cups flour

2 teaspoons baking powder

½ teaspoon cinnamon

In medium bowl blend butter with sugar. Beat in egg, then coffee and chocolate. In small bowl mix well flour, baking powder, and cinnamon; stir into chocolate mixture until well blended. Drop by rounded teaspoonfuls 1 inch apart on greased baking sheets; flatten slightly with fork tines.

Bake in preheated 350° F. oven 12 minutes, or until almost firm. Cool on racks.

Makes 24.

Giant Crisp Chocolate-Chip Cookies

2 cups flour

1 teaspoon baking soda

1 teaspoon salt

1 cup unsalted butter or margarine, softened

1½ cups sugar

1 egg

1 teaspoon vanilla extract

1 package (12 ounces) semisweet chocolate pieces (2 cups)

1 cup chopped nuts

Mix flour, baking soda, and salt; set aside.

In large bowl cream butter until fluffy. Gradually beat in sugar until light. Beat in egg and vanilla until blended and fluffy. Stir in flour mixture, chocolate, and nuts until well mixed. Shape in 2-inch balls; place 3 inches apart on ungreased cookie sheets (6 on each sheet).

Bake on middle rack in preheated 350° F. oven 20 to 23 minutes, or until golden and edges are lightly browned. Cool completely on cookie sheet. Store covered in dry, cool place.

Makes twenty-one 4-inch cookies.

Saucepan Fudge Cookies

¼ cup unsalted butter or margarine

3 squares (1 ounce each) unsweetened chocolate

1 cup sugar plus 3 tablespoons, divided

2 eggs

1 teaspoon vanilla extract

½ cup chopped nuts

1 cup flour mixed with 1 teaspoon baking powder and
    ¼ teaspoon salt

In 3-quart heavy saucepan over low heat stir butter and chocolate until melted and smooth; cool. Stir in 1 cup sugar, eggs, vanilla, and nuts until well blended. Stir in flour mixture until well blended. Cover and chill 1½ to 2 hours, or until dough is firm enough to shape.

Roll in 1½-inch balls; roll balls in remaining 3 tablespoons sugar. Place 2 inches apart on ungreased cookie sheet.

Bake in preheated 300° F. oven 20 minutes, or until crackled on top and slightly firm to touch. Immediately remove to rack to cool. Store tightly covered in cool place up to 1 week. Can be frozen.

Makes 25.

Giant Chocolate Crackles

2 cups flour

2 teaspoons baking powder

½ teaspoon salt

½ cup unsalted butter or margarine, softened

2 cups sugar

4 squares (1 ounce each) unsweetened chocolate, melted and cooled

4 eggs

2 teaspoons vanilla extract

Mix well flour, baking powder, and salt; set aside.

In large bowl of mixer cream butter and sugar until light. Beat in chocolate until blended. Add eggs and vanilla; beat until light and fluffy. Gradually stir in flour mixture until well blended. Chill dough well.

Using heaping tablespoonfuls of dough, shape in balls. Place 3 inches apart on greased cookie sheets.

Bake in preheated 350° F. oven 25 minutes, or until top of cookie springs back when lightly pressed with finger. Remove to racks to cool.

Makes about 24 large cookies.

Chocolate-Almond Spritz Cookies

½ cup unsalted butter or margarine, softened

1 cup sugar

1 egg

2 squares (1 ounce each) unsweetened chocolate, melted and cooled

2 teaspoons milk

1 teaspoon vanilla extract

1¼ cups flour

½ cup ground roasted almonds

½ teaspoon salt

Confectioners' sugar (optional)

In large bowl of mixer cream together butter and sugar until fluffy. Beat in egg until light and fluffy. Add chocolate, milk, and vanilla. Blend well. Gradually stir in flour, almonds, and salt until well blended. Chill at least 2 hours.

Press through cookie press in desired shapes about 1 inch apart on ungreased cookie sheets.

Bake in preheated 350° F. oven 8 to 10 minutes, or until top springs back when pressed lightly with fingertips. Cool on cookie sheets 1 minute; remove to racks to cool completely. Sprinkle with confectioners' sugar.

Store in airtight container in cool, dry place. Will keep about 2 weeks. Makes about 87.

Chocolate Refrigerator Cookies

1 cup flour, plus 2 tablespoons

3 tablespoons cocoa

½ cup unsalted butter or margarine, softened

6 tablespoons sugar

1 teaspoon vanilla extract

⅛ teaspoon salt

Slivered almonds

Mix flour and cocoa until well blended; set aside.

In large bowl of mixer cream butter, sugar, vanilla, and salt until fluffy. Gradually stir in flour mixture until blended. On lightly floured surface shape dough in 9-inch roll. Wrap airtight; chill several hours or overnight.

Cut in ¼-inch slices. Place 1 inch apart on lightly greased cookie sheet. Press almond sliver on each.

Bake in preheated 350° F. oven 12 minutes. Remove to rack to cool.

Makes about 36.

Chocolate-Nut Shortbread

2 squares (1 ounce each) unsweetened chocolate
1 cup unsalted butter or margarine, softened
1½ cups confectioners' sugar
2¼ cups flour
½ cup chopped walnuts
1 egg white mixed with 1 tablespoon water
Chocolate sprinkles or finely chopped nuts for
    garnish (optional)

Melt chocolate in top of double boiler or heatproof bowl set over simmering water; cool.

In large bowl cream butter; blend in cooled chocolate. Stir in sugar, flour, and walnuts (dough will be crumbly). Press in a long rectangle, 2 inches wide and 2 inches high. Brush with egg-white mixture; roll in sprinkles to coat sides well. Wrap tight; chill 4 hours, or until firm.

With sharp, thin knife, using sawing motion, slice ⅜ inch thick. Place slices 1 inch apart on ungreased baking sheet.

Bake in preheated 375° F. oven 10 to 12 minutes, or until edges are firm. Remove to rack to cool.

Makes 36.

Bitter-Chocolate Biscuits

These superb cookies contain no leavening and, when baked, have an almost brownielike texture.

    ½ cup unsalted butter, softened

    1 cup sugar

    Dash of salt

    1 egg

    4 squares (1 ounce each) unsweetened chocolate

    1½ cups all-purpose flour

    1 teaspoon vanilla extract

Cream butter and sugar until light. Add salt and egg and beat until fluffy. Melt chocolate over hot water or very low heat; add to first mixture and blend well. Add remaining ingredients and mix well. Chill until firm enough to roll.

On floured board with floured rolling pin, roll small amounts of dough at a time to ¼-inch thickness. Cut with round 1½- to 2-inch cutter, and put 1 inch apart on ungreased cookie sheet.

Bake in 375° F. oven about 7 minutes. Remove to cake racks to cool. Store airtight.

Makes about 4 dozen.

Chocolate Sandwich Cookies

1 recipe Chocolate Refrigerator Cookie dough (page 71)

Almond-Mocha Filling
⅓ cup unsalted butter or margarine, softened

¾ cup plus 1 tablespoon confectioners' sugar, divided

1 egg yolk

½ teaspoon almond extract

1 tablespoon cocoa

½ teaspoon instant coffee

1 tablespoon boiling water

¼ cup toasted almonds, chopped fine

Bring chilled dough to room temperature; with serrated knife cut in ³⁄₁₆-inch slices. Place 1 inch apart on lightly greased cookie sheet. Bake in preheated 350° F. oven 10 minutes until firm to touch. Remove to racks to cool.

Meanwhile, in small bowl of mixer, cream butter and ¾ cup confectioners' sugar until fluffy. Beat in egg yolk and almond extract; set aside. Mix cocoa, coffee, and water. Beat in creamed mixture until well blended. Fold in almonds.

Spread heaping measuring-teaspoon of filling on bottoms of half the cookies. Top with remaining cookies. Sift remaining 1 tablespoon confectioners' sugar on cookies. Store in cool place.

Makes about 22.

Chocolate Macaroons

2 egg whites, slightly beaten

¾ cup sugar

¼ teaspoon almond extract

¾ cup whole blanched almonds, ground or chopped in blender (makes about 1 cup)

½ cup fine dry bread crumbs

1 cup milk-chocolate pieces

1 square (1 ounce) unsweetened chocolate

3 tablespoons unsalted butter

1 egg, beaten

1 teaspoon vanilla extract

4 squares (1 ounce each) semisweet chocolate, melted

Pistachio or almond slivers

Combine and mix well first 5 ingredients. Chill ½ hour. Shape dough in balls with hands, using a rounded measuring-teaspoonful for each. If dough sticks to hands, rinse hands in cold water. Put balls on well-buttered and flour-dusted baking sheet.

Bake in preheated 300° F. oven 12 to 15 minutes, or until golden but still chewy (do not overbake). Cool 2 minutes, then remove to rack to cool completely.

Combine next 3 ingredients in top of double boiler and melt over hot water. Remove from water and beat in egg and vanilla until shiny and smooth. Chill, until stiff enough to spread.

Put a measuring-teaspoonful of chocolate mixture in center of flat side of macaroons, and mound with a small spatula. Chill 15 minutes.

Glaze chocolate mixture with melted chocolate, using a small spatula. Garnish with nut slivers before glaze hardens. Store airtight in cool place.

Makes about 3 dozen.

Chocolate-Filled and -Coated Macaroons

2 egg whites

¾ cup sugar

1¼ teaspoons vanilla extract, divided

1 cup blanched almonds, ground or chopped fine in blender or
    food processor (makes about 1¼ cups)

¼ cup fine dry bread crumbs

1 cup milk-chocolate pieces

1 square (1 ounce) unsweetened chocolate

3 tablespoons unsalted butter or margarine

1 egg, beaten

4 squares (1 ounce each) semisweet chocolate, melted

Toasted chopped almonds

In bowl, with whisk, beat egg whites slightly (until foamy). Fold in sugar, ¼ teaspoon vanilla, ground almonds, and bread crumbs. Chill ½ hour.

Using rounded measuring-teaspoonfuls, shape dough in balls. (If sticky, rinse hands in cold water.) Place balls 1 inch apart on well-greased, floured cookie sheet.

Bake in preheated 300° F. oven 18 to 20 minutes, or until golden on bottom but still slightly moist (do not overbake). Cool 2 minutes; remove to rack to cool completely.

In top of double boiler over simmering water melt milk chocolate, unsweetened chocolate, and butter without stirring. Remove from water; beat until smooth. Beat in egg and remaining 1 teaspoon vanilla until smooth and shiny. Chill until stiff enough to spread, about 15 minutes.

Mound measuring-teaspoonful of chocolate mixture on flat side of each macaroon, smoothing with small spatula. Chill 15 minutes.

With small spatula, quickly spread melted semisweet chocolate over chocolate-topped macaroons. Garnish with chopped almonds before glaze hardens. Store airtight in cool place.

Makes 36.

A Batch of Brownies and Other Chocolate Bars

Here they are, an assortment of bars and brownies that will fill your home with the sweet smell of chocolate. What is more satisfying than creating a pan full of nutty deep, dark, and delicious brownies and eating them warm right out of the pan?

This chapter includes a selection of absolutely indescribable brownies that will make your mouth water when you read the recipes. You'll find Chocolate-Syrup Brownies, Dark-Chocolate Supreme Brownies, Rich 'n' Moist Marble Brownies, and Superrich Double-Frosted Brownies—all made with the richest ingredients and all kitchen-tested by the *Woman's Day* experts.

Chocolate-Banana Bars

1 package (6 ounces) semisweet chocolate pieces

1 cup minus 2 tablespoons all-purpose flour

¾ cup sugar

¼ teaspoon salt

¾ teaspoon cinnamon

½ teaspoon baking powder

¼ teaspoon baking soda

1 cup mashed ripe bananas (about 2 medium)

¼ cup unsalted butter or margarine, softened

1 egg

2 tablespoons milk

1 cup chopped nuts

Brown-Velvet Frosting

Melt chocolate over hot water. Mix flour, sugar, salt, cinnamon, baking powder, and soda and set aside.

In large bowl of mixer beat bananas and butter until blended. Beat in egg. Add flour mixture and milk and mix well. Stir in chocolate and nuts. Spread in greased and floured 13 x 9 x 2-inch pan.

Bake in preheated 350° F. oven about 25 minutes. Cool in pan, then spread with frosting. Cut in bars.

Makes thirty-two 2 x 1½-inch bars.

Brown-Velvet Frosting

1 package (6 ounces) semisweet chocolate pieces

2 tablespoons unsalted butter or margarine

1½ cups confectioners' sugar

¼ cup milk

¼ teaspoon vanilla extract

⅛ teaspoon salt

Melt chocolate and butter in heavy saucepan. Remove from heat and beat in remaining ingredients.

Chocolate-Chip Bars

2 cups flour

1 teaspoon baking soda

½ cup unsalted butter or margarine, softened

½ cup granulated sugar

1½ cups packed brown sugar, divided

2 eggs, separated

1 tablespoon water

1 teaspoon vanilla extract

1 package (6 ounces) semisweet chocolate pieces

Stir together flour and baking soda; set aside.

Cream butter, granulated sugar, ½ cup brown sugar, egg yolks, water, and vanilla until light. Fold flour mixture into creamed mixture until well blended. On cookie sheet, with lightly floured fingertips, shape dough in 12 x 8-inch rectangle (it will spread considerably during baking). Sprinkle on chocolate pieces and press slightly into dough. Beat egg whites until stiff. Gradually beat in remaining 1 cup brown sugar until stiff meringue forms. Spread evenly over dough.

Bake on lowest rack in preheated 325° F. oven 30 minutes, or until meringue is golden brown and rectangle is crisp at edges. Remove to rack; cool. Cut in 2 x 1-inch bars.

Makes 72.

Fudgy Oatmeal Squares

1 cup instant rolled oats

1½ cups boiling water

1 cup flour

1½ cups granulated sugar

½ cup cocoa

1 teaspoon baking soda

½ teaspoon salt

½ cup shortening

1 teaspoon vanilla extract

2 eggs

Confectioners' sugar (optional)

Stir together oats and water; set aside.

In large bowl of mixer stir together flour, granulated sugar, cocoa, soda, and salt. Add shortening, oat mixture, and vanilla; beat at low speed just until mixed, then beat at medium speed 2 minutes, scraping bowl frequently. Add eggs; beat at medium speed 2 minutes, scraping bowl occasionally. Pour into greased 13 x 9 x 2-inch pan.

Bake in preheated 350° F. oven 35 minutes, or until pick inserted in center comes out clean. Cool in pan 10 minutes, then turn out on rack and cool completely. Sprinkle with confectioners' sugar. Cut in squares.

Makes about 24.

Chocolate Peanut-Butter Bars

1 cup flour

1 cup quick-cooking rolled oats

½ teaspoon baking soda

¼ teaspoon salt

½ cup unsalted butter or margarine, softened

1 cup packed brown sugar

1 egg

⅓ cup creamy peanut butter

1 teaspoon vanilla extract

6 squares (1 ounce each) semisweet chocolate

½ cup confectioners' sugar

3 to 4 tablespoons milk

¼ cup chopped peanuts (optional)

Mix flour, oats, soda, and salt; set aside.

In large bowl of mixer cream butter, brown sugar, and egg until fluffy. Blend in ⅓ cup peanut butter and vanilla. Stir in flour mixture. Spread in greased 13 x 9 x 2-inch pan.

Bake in preheated 350° F. oven 20 to 25 minutes, or until pick inserted in center comes out clean. Sprinkle immediately with chocolate; let stand 5 minutes to melt. Spread melted chocolate over top. Blend confectioners' sugar, ¼ cup peanut butter, and enough milk to make a thin icing; drizzle over chocolate. Sprinkle with peanuts. Cool in pan.

Makes about 32 bars.

Black-Pepper Brownies

¾ cup unsalted butter or margarine, softened

1¼ cups packed brown sugar

1 teaspoon instant coffee

1 teaspoon black pepper

1 teaspoon vanilla extract

⅛ teaspoon salt

3 eggs

4 squares (1 ounce each) unsweetened chocolate, melted and cooled

¾ cup flour

1 cup walnuts or pecans, chopped coarse

In large bowl cream butter. Add sugar, coffee, pepper, vanilla, and salt; beat until well blended, scraping bowl. Add eggs one at a time, beating after each only until incorporated. Slowly beat in chocolate, then flour, scraping bowl and beating only until blended. Stir in nuts. Turn into greased, foil-lined 9-inch-square pan; smooth top.

Bake in lower third of preheated 375° F. oven 25 to 30 minutes, or until pick inserted in center comes out barely moist. Remove from oven; cool in pan 15 minutes. Remove from pan; peel off foil, and cool completely on rack. Chill slightly before cutting.

Makes 32 small brownies or 16 cake squares.

Bourbon Brownies

⅓ cup unsalted butter

2 squares (1 ounce each) unsweetened chocolate

½ teaspoon vanilla extract

1 cup sugar

2 eggs

¾ cup all-purpose flour

¼ teaspoon salt

About 3 tablespoons bourbon

Granulated sugar

Melt butter and chocolate in saucepan over low heat, stirring; cool. Beat in vanilla and sugar. Add eggs one at a time, beating well after each. Mix flour and salt, and stir into chocolate mixture. Spread in greased 8-inch-square pan.

Bake in 325° F. oven about 25 minutes; cool. When thoroughly cooled, crumble brownies into bowl. Sprinkle with bourbon; mix in with fingers. Shape in 1-inch balls or logs about 1 inch long. Roll in sugar. Store in airtight container for a day before serving or giving.

Makes 3 to 3½ dozen.

Note: To give as a festive Christmas gift, put in metal star mold and cover with foil. Trim with greens and ornament.

Chocolate-Syrup Brownies

½ cup unsalted butter or margarine

1 cup sugar

3 eggs

1 cup all-purpose flour

¾ cup canned chocolate syrup

1 teaspoon vanilla extract

1 cup chopped nuts

Cocoa Frosting

Nut halves

Cream butter and sugar together. Add eggs one at a time, beating after each. Add remaining ingredients, except frosting and nut halves, and mix well. Spread in buttered 9-inch-square pan.

Bake in 350° F. oven about 40 minutes. Cool in pan on cake rack. Spread with frosting. When firm, cut in 2¼-inch squares. Press a nut half in center of each.

Makes 16.

Cocoa Frosting

1 tablespoon unsalted butter or margarine

3 tablespoons milk

1½ cups confectioners' sugar

Dash of salt

¼ cup unsweetened cocoa

½ teaspoon vanilla extract

Heat butter and milk until butter is melted. Mix sugar, salt, and cocoa. Add milk, stirring to blend. Then add vanilla and beat with spoon 1 minute or until smooth.

Dark-Chocolate Supreme Brownies

4 eggs

2 cups sugar

⅓ cup vegetable oil

4 squares (1 ounce each) unsweetened chocolate, melted and
    cooled, or 4 envelopes no-melt chocolate

2 teaspoons vanilla extract

1⅓ cups all-purpose flour

1 teaspoon baking powder

½ teaspoon salt

1 cup chopped nuts

Beat eggs until thick and lemon-colored. Gradually add sugar and beat
until well blended. Stir in oil, chocolate, and vanilla. Mix dry ingredients
together and add to mixture, blending well. Stir in nuts and spread in
buttered 13 x 9 x 2-inch pan.

    Bake in moderate 350° F. oven 25 to 30 minutes. Cool in pan on cake
rack. Cut in 2-inch squares.

    Makes 24.

Chocolate Whole-Wheat Brownies

½ cup whole-wheat flour

½ teaspoon baking powder

¼ teaspoon salt

½ cup unsalted butter or margarine, softened

⅔ cup sugar

2 squares (1 ounce each) unsweetened chocolate,
    melted and cooled

2 eggs

1 teaspoon vanilla extract

¾ cup chopped nuts, divided

Mix flour, baking powder, and salt; set aside.

Cream butter and sugar until fluffy. Beat in chocolate, eggs, and vanilla. Stir in flour mixture and ½ cup nuts. Spread in greased 8-inch-square pan. Sprinkle with remaining nuts.

Bake in preheated 350° F. oven 20 minutes, or until brownies pull away from sides of pan and pick inserted in center comes out clean. Cool in pan on rack. Cut in 2-inch squares.

Makes 16.

Superrich Double-Frosted Brownies

5 squares (1 ounce each) unsweetened chocolate, divided

½ cup unsalted butter or margarine

2 eggs

1 cup sugar

1 teaspoon vanilla extract

½ cup flour mixed with ¼ teaspoon salt and ½ cup
  chopped nuts

Frosting

Melt 2 squares chocolate and butter in heavy saucepan; cool.

In bowl beat eggs until blended; add sugar and mix well. Stir in chocolate mixture, vanilla, and flour mixture. Spread in greased 11 x 7 x 1½-inch pan.

Bake in preheated 350° F. oven 20 to 25 minutes. Cool in pan on rack.

Spread with Frosting. Melt remaining 3 squares chocolate; spread over Frosting. Chill several hours or until firm. Bring to room temperature, then cut in squares.

Makes 15.

Frosting

Mix 1½ cups sugar, ⅓ cup unsalted butter or margarine, and ½ cup half-and-half in heavy medium saucepan. Bring to boil, then cook over moderate heat *without stirring* until small amount of mixture forms soft ball when dropped in ice water (236° F. on candy thermometer). Cool in pan of cold water until lukewarm. Add 1 teaspoon vanilla extract; beat until creamy and of spreading consistency.

Rich 'n' Moist Marble Brownies

1 cup unsalted butter or margarine, softened

1½ teaspoons vanilla extract

2 cups sugar

4 eggs

1¾ cups flour

½ teaspoon salt

2 cups coarsely chopped nuts

2 squares (1 ounce each) unsweetened chocolate,
   melted and cooled

Velvety Chocolate Frosting

Cream butter, vanilla, and sugar until light and fluffy. Add eggs one at a time, beating well after each. Add flour and salt, and mix until blended. Stir in nuts. Divide batter in half and add chocolate to half. Drop batters alternately by heaping teaspoonfuls into greased 13 x 9 x 2-inch pan lined on bottom with wax paper. Press with spoon to smooth top and run knife through batter several times to marbleize.

Bake in preheated 350° F. oven about 45 minutes. Turn out on cake rack and peel off paper at once. Cool and frost. At serving time cut into squares.

Makes about 24.

Velvety Chocolate Frosting

¼ cup hot water

2¼ cups confectioners' sugar

4 squares (1 ounce each) unsweetened chocolate, melted

4 egg yolks

¼ cup unsalted butter or margarine, melted

1 teaspoon vanilla extract

Add hot water and sugar to chocolate and mix well. Add egg yolks one at a time, beating well after each. Slowly add butter, then vanilla, and beat until smooth. If too thin to spread immediately, let stand a few minutes to thicken.

Makes enough for 13 x 9-inch rectangle or two 8-inch cake layers.

Chewy Thin Chocolate Brownie Bars

1 square (1 ounce) unsweetened chocolate
¼ cup unsalted butter or margarine
½ cup sugar
1 egg
¼ cup flour
1 teaspoon vanilla extract
⅛ teaspoon salt
⅓ cup chopped walnuts, pecans, or filberts

Melt chocolate and butter in heavy saucepan over low heat (mixture should be melted but not hot). Remove from heat; stir in sugar. Add egg, flour, vanilla, and salt; mix well. Spread evenly in greased 13 x 9 x 2-inch pan. Sprinkle with walnuts.

Bake in preheated 400° F. oven 12 minutes, or until top is firm to touch. Cool slightly; cut in bars (must be cut while quite hot). When cool, remove from pan to racks to crisp.

Makes 24 to 30.

Chocolate-Walnut Squares

½ cup unsalted butter or margarine

¾ cup sifted confectioners' sugar

4 eggs, separated

3 squares (1 ounce each) semisweet chocolate,
   melted and cooled

1 cup walnuts, ground

2 tablespoons flour

½ teaspoon vanilla extract

Walnut Filling

Chocolate Glaze

25 walnut halves

Cream butter until very light. Add sugar a little at a time, beating well after each addition. Beat egg yolks until light and lemon-colored, then beat into butter mixture. Add chocolate, walnuts, flour, and vanilla, and mix well. Beat egg whites until stiff and fold gently into batter. Turn into 2 well-greased 8-inch-square pans.

Bake in preheated 350° F. oven about 20 minutes. Cool a few minutes, then turn out on cake rack. When cool, prepare filling and spread between layers. Cut in 1½-inch squares. Spread top and sides with glaze and top each square with a walnut half before glaze sets.

Makes 25.

Walnut Filling

1 square (1 ounce) semisweet chocolate

3 tablespoons sugar

1 cup walnuts, ground

¼ cup milk

2 tablespoons unsalted butter or margarine

½ teaspoon vanilla extract

Melt chocolate in top of double boiler over hot (not boiling) water. Add sugar, walnuts, and milk and cook, stirring until thickened. Remove from heat. Add butter and vanilla and beat until thoroughly cooled.

Chocolate Glaze

1 package (6 ounces) semisweet chocolate pieces
2 tablespoons unsalted butter or margarine
2 tablespoons light corn syrup
3 tablespoons milk

Melt chocolate and butter in top of double boiler over hot (not boiling) water. Stir in corn syrup and milk and beat until smooth.

Puddings, Mousses, Soufflés, and Other Delights

Chocolate desserts are the ultimate ending to a glorious meal. The light, delicate elegance of a chocolate mousse is the perfect palate-pleaser after a spicy dish. The old-fashioned downright deliciousness of Double-Chocolate Ice Cream is beyond comparison. And the sweet smoothness of Chocolate Bavarian Cream is absolute heaven on earth.

Here are recipes for some of your favorites along with recipes for desserts that were once special treats when out on the town. Your favorite family meal can be made superspecial when it is topped by superfudgy, endlessly rich Chocolate-Crumb Pudding. And within these pages is the quintessential dessert, the ultimate in contrasts, a joy to look at, a challenge to prepare, an absolute dream to eat—Twin Baked Alaskas with Chocolate-Rum Sauce.

These chocolate desserts are what fantasies are made of.

Steamed Chocolate Pudding

⅓ cup unsalted butter or margarine

2 squares (1 ounce each) unsweetened chocolate

1 egg

1 cup sugar

1 teaspoon vanilla extract

1¼ cups flour

1 teaspoon baking soda

¼ teaspoon salt

1 cup milk

Sweetened whipped cream or ice cream (optional)

In small saucepan over low heat stir butter and chocolate until melted and smooth; cool slightly. In medium bowl beat egg, sugar, and vanilla just until blended. Gradually beat in chocolate mixture until blended. Mix well flour, baking soda, and salt; beat into chocolate mixture alternately with milk, beating just until smooth. Pour into a well-greased and floured 1½-quart mold or six 1-cup molds. Cover tightly with lid or foil secured with rubber bands. Place on rack in large kettle; add boiling water halfway up sides of mold (see Note).

Steam large mold 1 hour, individual molds 30 to 40 minutes, or until pick inserted in center comes out clean. Remove from kettle; cool on rack 10 minutes. Unmold. Best served warm with whipped cream.

Makes 6 servings.

Note: Individual molds may be steamed in a large skillet with tight-fitting dome lid.

Chocolate-Crumb Pudding

This has a fantastic texture and glorious, full chocolate taste. A ruby port goes beautifully with it.

  1½ cups fine soft bread crumbs, preferably from French-style
     or firm white bread
  6 tablespoons unsalted butter or margarine, divided
  2 squares (1 ounce each) unsweetened baking chocolate
  2 eggs
  1 egg yolk
  1 cup plus 2½ tablespoons sugar, divided
  1½ cups milk
  ½ teaspoon vanilla extract
  Dash of salt

In large heavy skillet over medium heat sauté crumbs in 5 tablespoons butter until crisp and deep golden; set aside.

In top of double boiler over simmering water, or small heavy saucepan over low heat, melt chocolate and remaining butter; set aside.

In bowl slightly beat eggs and yolk; beat in 1 cup plus 2 tablespoons sugar. Gradually beat in chocolate mixture, then milk, vanilla, and salt. Stir in crumbs. Pour into 1-quart buttered soufflé dish or other baking dish. Set in shallow pan; add hot water to come 1 inch up sides of dish. Sprinkle remaining sugar over top.

Bake in preheated 350° F. oven 50 to 65 minutes, or until knife inserted in center comes out clean. Cool on rack to lukewarm or room temperature. Spoon to serve.

Makes 5 servings.

The Ultimate Chocolate Mousse

1 tablespoon unsalted butter

3 squares (1 ounce each) unsweetened chocolate

2 eggs, separated

½ cup sugar, divided

2 teaspoons dark rum

1 teaspoon cold strong coffee

1 cup heavy cream, whipped

In small heavy saucepan over low heat melt butter and chocolate. Stir until smooth; set aside.

In small bowl of mixer beat egg whites until foamy. Gradually beat in ¼ cup sugar until stiff peaks form; set aside.

In large bowl of mixer beat egg yolks with remaining sugar until lemon-colored and light. Beat in rum and coffee. With rubber spatula fold in chocolate mixture, then gently fold in egg-white mixture and whipped cream just to blend. Spoon into 4 individual serving dishes. (If desired, reserve about 1 cup mousse, put into pastry bag with fluted tip, and form rosettes on servings.) Chill several hours or overnight.

Serves 4.

Mocha Mousse

4 squares (1 ounce each) sweet cooking chocolate
¼ cup brandy
1 egg yolk
1 teaspoon instant coffee, preferably espresso
1 cup heavy cream
2 tablespoons sugar
4 pieces bittersweet chocolate, for garnish (optional)

In small heavy saucepan over low heat melt sweet chocolate with brandy, stirring until smooth. Remove from heat; stir in egg yolk and coffee until well blended. Set aside to cool while beating cream with sugar until stiff. Gently but thoroughly fold in chocolate mixture. Spoon into dessert dish or 4 stemmed glasses. Garnish with bittersweet chocolate. Chill at least 30 minutes.

Makes 4 servings.

Frozen Chocolate Mousse

1 envelope unflavored gelatin
1 cup milk
2 squares (1 ounce each) unsweetened chocolate
¾ cup sugar
2 teaspoons vanilla extract
2 cups heavy cream, softly whipped
Unsweetened whipped cream (optional)

In heavy medium saucepan sprinkle gelatin over milk; let stand 5 minutes to soften. Add chocolate and sugar. Stir over moderate heat until chocolate melts and is well blended, using a whisk if necessary. Chill to lukewarm. Stir in vanilla; fold in softly whipped cream. Turn into 1-quart mold. Freeze until firm. To serve, unmold; serve with unsweetened whipped cream.

Makes 6 generous servings.

Blender Chocolate-Orange Mousse

1 teaspoon grated orange rind

¼ cup firmly packed light brown sugar

2 egg yolks

2 whole eggs

6 squares (1 ounce each) semisweet chocolate,
    melted and cooled

3 tablespoons orange juice

1 cup heavy cream

Decoration: whipped cream or whipped topping and
    orange-peel slivers

Combine first 4 ingredients in blender and whirl until light and foamy. Add chocolate, orange juice, and cream. Continue to whirl until well blended. Pour into small individual serving dishes and chill until set. Garnish with a swirl of whipped cream and a piece of orange peel.

    Makes 5 servings.

Chilled Chocolate Soufflé

⅓ cup Dutch-process cocoa

⅓ cup sugar

1 envelope unflavored gelatin

1¾ cups milk, divided

1 teaspoon vanilla extract

2 egg whites, at room temperature

⅛ teaspoon salt

½ cup heavy cream, whipped

In small saucepan mix cocoa, sugar, and gelatin. Gradually stir in ½ cup milk until smooth and blended. Stir over low heat about 3 minutes, or until gelatin dissolves. Remove from heat; stir in remaining cups milk and vanilla. Chill until mixture mounds slightly when dropped from spoon.

    Beat egg whites with salt until stiff but not dry. Fold in whipped cream and carefully fold into gelatin mixture. Chill at least 1 hour.

    Makes 4 servings.

Frozen Chocolate-Pecan Mousse Ring

2 eggs, separated

¼ teaspoon salt

½ cup sugar

1 teaspoon vanilla extract

1 cup heavy cream, whipped

¾ cup toasted chopped pecans

1 square (1 ounce) unsweetened chocolate, chopped fine

2 teaspoons oil

3 squares (1 ounce each) semisweet chocolate, melted

Pecan halves, for garnish (optional)

In small bowl of mixer at medium speed beat egg whites and salt until soft peaks form. Gradually beat in sugar until mixture is glossy and stiff peaks form; set aside.

In large bowl beat egg yolks and vanilla with fork until well blended. Fold in about one-third of egg-white mixture until well blended. Add remaining egg-white mixture, cream, pecans, and chopped chocolate; fold to blend well. Line 4-cup ring mold or mixing bowl with plastic wrap. Fill with mixture; smooth top; cover and freeze until firm (or overnight).

Blend oil into melted chocolate. Cool. Run small spatula around tube in ring mold. Invert mousse on chilled serving plate. Peel off plastic wrap. Drizzle chocolate-oil mixture over mousse. Return to freezer until serving time. Before serving, decorate with pecan halves, if desired.

Makes 8 servings.

Mocha-Rum Soufflé

2 envelopes unflavored gelatin

1 cup sugar, divided

¼ teaspoon salt

1 tablespoon instant coffee

4 eggs, separated

1½ cups milk

1 package (12 ounces) semisweet chocolate pieces (2 cups)

½ cup light rum

1 teaspoon vanilla extract

2 cups heavy cream, whipped

¼ cup finely chopped nuts

In saucepan stir together gelatin, ½ cup sugar, salt, and coffee. Beat egg yolks and milk; stir into gelatin mixture. Add chocolate and stir over low heat until gelatin dissolves and chocolate melts, 7 to 8 minutes. Remove from heat and beat with mixer or rotary beater to blend mixture thoroughly. Stir in rum and vanilla; chill, stirring occasionally, until mixture mounds slightly when dropped from spoon.

Beat egg whites until stiff but not dry. Gradually add remaining sugar, and continue to beat. Fold gelatin mixture into egg-white mixture, then gently fold in whipped cream. Turn into 1½-quart soufflé dish or casserole fitted with 3-inch collar (see Note); chill until firm. Garnish with chopped nuts.

Makes 12 to 15 servings.

Note: To make collar, double-fold foil in strip 3 inches wide and long enough to go around soufflé dish with 2-inch overlap. Wrap around outside of dish so that foil extends about 2 inches above rim; fasten with tape. Brush inside of strip with oil. When soufflé is ready to serve, loosen tape and gently remove collar from dish.

Hot Chocolate-Mint Soufflés

5 tablespoons granulated sugar, divided
1 teaspoon cornstarch
Dash of salt
⅓ cup milk
⅓ cup semisweet mint-flavored chocolate pieces
2 eggs, separated
Confectioners' sugar

Lightly grease two 10-ounce custard cups or two 2-cup soufflé dishes. Sprinkle each with ½ tablespoon granulated sugar; tap out excess.

In medium saucepan mix 2 tablespoons granulated sugar with cornstarch and salt. Gradually stir in milk. Stir over medium heat until mixture thickens and boils, about 3 minutes. Stir in chocolate-mint pieces until they melt; set aside to cool slightly. In medium bowl beat egg yolks slightly; beat in small amount of chocolate mixture. Beat yolk mixture into chocolate in saucepan; cool (see Note).

Beat egg whites until foamy; gradually add remaining granulated sugar, and continue beating until stiff peaks form. Fold into chocolate mixture. Pour into prepared dishes.

Bake in preheated 375° F. oven 20 to 25 minutes (center of soufflé should wiggle slightly). Sprinkle with confectioners' sugar. Serve immediately.

Makes 2 servings.

Note: Can be prepared this far in advance; let stand up to 1½ hours. Beat and fold in egg whites just before baking.

Chocolate Bavarian Cream

¾ cup sugar, divided

¼ cup cocoa

1 envelope unflavored gelatin

1½ cups milk

3 eggs, separated, at room temperature

1 teaspoon vanilla extract

¾ cup heavy cream

In top of double boiler over simmering water, or in heavy saucepan over medium-low heat, mix well ½ cup sugar, cocoa, and gelatin; stir in milk. Cook just to boiling. Stir ½ cup cocoa mixture into egg yolks, then stir into pan mixture. Cook and stir until mixture coats metal spoon, 10 to 15 minutes. Remove from heat; stir in vanilla. Cool, then chill until mixture mounds when dropped from spoon, stirring occasionally.

In small bowl of mixer beat egg whites and remaining sugar until stiff peaks form; set aside. In another bowl whip cream until stiff peaks form. Fold egg-white mixture and cream into chilled custard. Spoon into chilled 6-cup mold. Chill until firm, 2 to 4 hours. Unmold on serving dish.

Makes 6 servings.

Pots de Crème au Chocolat

2 squares (1 ounce each) semisweet chocolate

¼ cup sugar

1 egg, beaten

⅛ teaspoon salt

¾ cup undiluted evaporated milk, divided

1 teaspoon vanilla extract

1 teaspoon lemon juice

Shaved chocolate

In top part of double boiler, melt chocolate over boiling water. Add sugar, egg, and salt and mix well. Stir in ¼ cup milk. Cook, stirring, over boiling water about 8 minutes. Remove from heat, stir in vanilla, and chill.

Pour remaining milk into smallest bowl of electric mixer and put in freezer with beaters. Chill until edges begin to freeze. Add lemon juice and beat at high speed until mixture is fluffy and forms peaks that hold their shape. Fold into cooled chocolate mixture. Pour into 6 pot-de-crème cups or small serving dishes and chill 3 hours. Serve with shaved chocolate.

Makes 6 servings.

Chocolate Blancmange

2½ cups milk, divided

2 squares (1 ounce each) unsweetened chocolate

1 teaspoon finely shredded orange peel

⅓ cup sugar

¼ cup cornstarch

¼ teaspoon salt

Canned or thawed frozen fruits (optional)

Light or heavy cream

In heavy saucepan heat 2 cups milk, chocolate, and orange peel over medium heat until chocolate melts, stirring occasionally. Blend sugar, cornstarch, and salt with remaining milk until smooth. Gradually stir into chocolate mixture; stir over low heat until smooth and thickened, about 5 minutes. Pour into custard cups or small molds; chill overnight. Unmold and serve with fruits and cream.

Makes five 4-ounce servings.

Chocolate Bread Pudding Supreme

1¼ cups finely crushed stale–bread crumbs

2 tablespoons unsalted butter or margarine, melted

½ cup sugar

2 squares (1 ounce each) unsweetened chocolate, melted

¼ teaspoon salt

2 cups milk, scalded

2 eggs

1 teaspoon vanilla extract

½ cup raisins

½ cup flaked coconut

3 tablespoons jam or jelly (any flavor)

12 marshmallows

Combine first 5 ingredients in bowl. Cover with milk, stir, and set aside to cool. Beat eggs and vanilla until fluffy and add to bread mixture. Stir in raisins and coconut. Pour into buttered shallow 1½-quart baking dish.

Bake in 350° F. oven 45 minutes. Remove from oven, spread with thin layer of jam or jelly, and arrange marshmallows on top. Put back in oven and bake 10 to 15 minutes, or until marshmallows are melted. Serve warm.

Makes 6 servings.

Double-Chocolate Ice Cream

½ cup sugar

1 tablespoon flour

⅛ teaspoon salt

2 eggs

1 cup half-and-half or milk

3 squares (1 ounce each) unsweetened chocolate, melted

2 teaspoons vanilla extract

1 cup heavy cream

3 squares (1 ounce each) semisweet chocolate, chopped coarse
   (in blender, food processor, or with sharp knife)

Place sugar, flour, salt, and eggs in heavy saucepan. Beat with wooden spoon until blended. Beat in half-and-half. Stir over low heat until mixture coats spoon and is smooth (do not overcook). Add melted chocolate and vanilla; beat until well blended and smooth; cool. Whip cream; fold into chocolate mixture to blend. Fold in chopped chocolate. Pour into chilled loaf pan, cover airtight, and freeze. Let stand at room temperature 15 minutes before serving.

Makes about 3 cups, or 6 servings.

Note: To make ice cream in electric ice-cream maker *do not whip cream.* Follow manufacturer's directions, setting freezer at coldest setting.

Chocolate-Raspberry Cream

2 cups heavy cream

½ teaspoon vanilla extract

4 squares (1 ounce each) sweet cooking chocolate,
   finely grated

3 cups fresh raspberries, or 2 packages (10 ounces each)
   thawed frozen raspberries, thoroughly drained

¼ cup sugar (omit if frozen berries are used)

Whip cream with vanilla. Add chocolate and blend thoroughly. Reserve a
few raspberries for garnish. Sprinkle sugar on remaining berries and fold
into cream. Spoon into individual serving dishes or large glass serving
bowl. Chill thoroughly. Before serving, decorate with reserved berries.
   Makes 6 to 8 servings.

Twin Baked Alaskas with Chocolate-Rum Sauce

Freeze one for a future special occasion.

    ½ cup unsalted butter or margarine
    3 squares (1 ounce each) unsweetened chocolate
    2 eggs
    1 cup sugar
    ½ teaspoon salt
    1 teaspoon vanilla extract
    ⅔ cup flour
    1 brick (½ gallon) coffee or other ice cream
    Meringue
    Chocolate-Rum Sauce

In small saucepan over low heat stir butter and chocolate until melted and smooth. Place in large bowl; cool slightly. Add eggs, sugar, and salt. Beat about 3 minutes or until thickened; beat in vanilla. Stir in flour just until blended. Spread evenly in well-greased 8- or 9-inch-square pan.

Bake in preheated 350° F. oven 30 minutes, or until pick inserted in center comes out clean. Cool in pan on rack 5 minutes, then invert on rack. Cool thoroughly; cut in half. Halve ice cream lengthwise. Put one-half on each cake half; place in freezer while making Meringue.

Place one Alaska on foil-lined cutting board. (Remaining Alaska can be wrapped in foil and frozen up to 3 weeks; see Note.) Spread Meringue to cover Alaska completely and seal in ice cream. Bake in preheated 425° F. oven 5 minutes, or until lightly browned. Serve immediately from board or serving dish in 1-inch slices with Chocolate-Rum Sauce.

Makes 8 servings.

Note: To prepare second Alaska, do not thaw. Follow directions for Meringue. Bake on foil-lined cookie sheet 7 to 8 minutes or until browned and cake thaws. Alaska may also be spread with Meringue and frozen up to 24 hours. Bake on foil-lined cookie sheet 5 to 7 minutes or until browned and cake thaws.

Meringue (for 1 Baked Alaska)
> 3 egg whites, at room temperature
> ¼ teaspoon cream of tartar
> ¼ teaspoon salt
> 6 tablespoons sugar
> ½ teaspoon vanilla extract

In small bowl beat whites until frothy. Add cream of tartar and salt; beat until soft peaks form. Gradually beat in sugar; continue beating until stiff peaks form. Beat in vanilla.

Chocolate-Rum Sauce (for 1 Baked Alaska)
> 2 squares (1 ounce each) unsweetened chocolate
> ½ cup water
> ½ cup sugar
> 2 tablespoons unsalted butter or margarine
> 3 tablespoons dark rum

In small saucepan over low heat stir chocolate and water until chocolate melts and mixture is smooth. Add sugar; stir until sugar dissolves. Remove from heat; stir in butter until melted. Stir in rum. Serve at room temperature.

Makes 1 cup.

Queen Bona's Dessert

8 ladyfingers, split
⅓ cup sherry, rum, or brandy
⅓ cup toasted blanched almonds
¼ cup unsalted butter
½ cup sugar
2 squares (1 ounce each) unsweetened chocolate
¼ cup milk
1 egg yolk
1 teaspoon vanilla extract
Walnut halves
Candied cherries

Place ladyfingers on large platter. Sprinkle with sherry. Ladyfingers must be only slightly moistened, or they will fall apart.

Grind almonds fine in blender or chop as fine as possible. Cream butter and sugar together until thoroughly blended. Melt chocolate in top part of double boiler over hot water. Beat together milk, egg yolk, and vanilla. Add mixture to chocolate in double boiler. Cook over simmering water until smooth, stirring constantly. Blend in butter-sugar mixture. Remove from heat. Beat with rotary beater until smooth. Cool.

With a broad spatula, place half of ladyfinger halves on serving dish. Take care not to break. Carefully pour a thin layer of chocolate cream over ladyfingers. Cover with remaining ladyfingers. Cover with remaining chocolate cream. Decorate with nuts and cherries. Chill thoroughly.

Makes 4 to 6 servings.

Classic Chocolate Eclairs

⅔ cup flour

2 tablespoons unsweetened cocoa

⅛ teaspoon salt

1 cup water

½ cup unsalted butter or margarine

4 eggs

Chocolate or vanilla ice cream

Basic Hot-Fudge Sauce (page 145)

Stir together flour, cocoa, and salt; set aside. In saucepan bring water and butter to boil. Reduce heat and quickly stir in flour mixture, beating vigorously with wooden spoon until mixture forms a soft ball. Remove from heat. With wooden spoon, beat in eggs one at a time, beating after each until mixture is thick, shiny, and smooth (an electric mixer can be used at low speed). Drop about 4 heaping teaspoonfuls batter in a line, to form ten 4 x 1½ x 1-inch strips 3 inches apart.

Bake in preheated 400° F. oven 30 minutes, or until puffed and light. Turn off heat and let eclairs dry in oven about 20 minutes. Remove to rack to cool.

With kitchen shears or sharp knife cut thin slice off top. Remove any unbaked dough inside eclairs. Fill each shell with ½ cup ice cream. Replace tops. Freeze in plastic bags or containers. Remove from freezer ½ hour before serving. Top with sauce.

Makes 10.

Chocolate-Filled Cream-Puff Ring

1 recipe Cream-Puff Paste
Chocolate Filling
Chocolate Glaze
Sliced almonds
Whipped cream (optional)

Butter a 9-inch circle on cookie sheet. Drop paste by ¼ cupfuls just inside circumference of circle so that it forms a ring. Or force paste through pastry bag fitted with wide-mouthed tube, forming 2 rings, one inside the other, to make base; continue piping remaining paste in layers until completely used.

Bake in preheated 400° F. oven 40 minutes, or until puffed and well browned. Cool on rack. A few hours before serving, carefully slice ring crosswise with long, sharp, thin-bladed knife and gently lift off top.

Fill with Chocolate Filling and replace top. Drizzle with Chocolate Glaze, then sprinkle with almonds. Chill several hours or until ready to serve. Serve with small dollop of whipped cream, if desired.

Makes 12 servings.

Cream-Puff Paste

1 cup water
½ cup unsalted butter or margarine
1 teaspoon sugar
¼ teaspoon salt
1 cup all-purpose flour
4 large eggs

Combine water, butter, sugar, and salt in heavy saucepan and bring to boil. Add flour all at once, then beat with wooden spoon over low heat 1 minute, or until mixture leaves sides of pan and forms a mixture that does not separate. Remove from heat and beat about 2 minutes to cool mixture slightly. Add eggs one at a time, beating after each until mixture has a satinlike sheen.

Chocolate Filling

> 1 cup unsalted butter or margarine, softened
> 1 cup sugar
> 4 squares (1 ounce each) unsweetened chocolate,
>   melted and cooled
> 2 teaspoons vanilla extract
> 6 eggs

Cream butter and sugar until light and fluffy. Beat in chocolate and vanilla, then add eggs one at a time, beating 2 minutes after each. Continue to beat until sugar is thoroughly dissolved, then chill.

Chocolate Glaze

In top of double boiler over hot (not boiling) water, melt 2 squares (1 ounce each) semisweet chocolate and 2 tablespoons unsalted butter or margarine, stirring to combine.

Black-Sea Islands

> 2 cups milk
> 3 eggs, separated
> ¼ teaspoon salt, divided
> 1 cup sugar, divided
> 2 tablespoons unsweetened cocoa, preferably Dutch process
> ¼ teaspoon cinnamon or 1 teaspoon vanilla extract
> Shaved chocolate for garnish (optional)

In large deep skillet over very low heat bring milk to a simmer. Meanwhile in medium bowl beat egg whites until foamy. Add ⅛ teaspoon salt and beat until soft peaks form. Gradually beat in ¾ cup sugar until meringue (egg-white mixture) is stiff but not dry. With large spoon scoop meringue into 5 egg-shaped puffs. Using a rubber spatula, gently push one puff at a time into hot milk. Cover with domed lid or foil; cook over low heat 4 to 5 minutes, or until meringues feel firm to the touch (do not overcook). Using a slotted spoon, immediately remove meringues to clean kitchen towel placed on a platter. Chill; strain milk and set aside.

In heavy 2-quart saucepan beat egg yolks with remaining sugar until lemon-colored. Beat in cocoa, cinnamon, and remaining salt until well blended. Stir in milk. Stir over low heat until mixture thickens slightly and coats a metal spoon. Pour into shallow 9- to 10-inch-diameter serving bowl. Cover with plastic wrap; chill. Just before serving, float meringues on custard; sprinkle with shaved chocolate or spoon a little custard on each. Serve in dessert bowls.

Makes 5 servings.

Chocolate Fondue with Cherry Dippers

2 tablespoons unsalted butter or margarine
1 package (6 ounces) semisweet chocolate pieces (1 cup)
1 can (14 ounces) sweetened condensed milk
1 teaspoon vanilla, peppermint, or orange extract
2 pounds sweet cherries with stems

In small heavy saucepan over low heat melt butter and chocolate, stirring occasionally. Stir in milk and extract. Stirring constantly, cook 5 minutes, or until smooth and hot. Serve warm from fondue pot, small saucepan, or heat-resistant bowl set over low to moderate heat. Surround with cherries for dipping.

Makes 8 servings.

Note: Refrigerated leftover fondue can be reheated over low heat; or served cold over ice cream.

Fudge and Confections

When that chocolate sweet tooth begins to beckon us to the kitchen, a batch of old-fashioned homemade chocolate fudge is the only thing that can satisfy it completely. Fudge is a special blend of ingredients that creates the perfect setting for chocolate richness to emerge. It will melt in your mouth and send a thrill through every single taste bud individually.

Here is a selection of fudge recipes that holds you by the hand so that you'll create the best fudge you've ever eaten. There's Quick Chocolate Fudge, Kneaded Chocolate Fudge, a special Christmas Fudge, Rich Chocolate Caramels, Double-Chocolate Cherry Bourbon Balls, and much more. All perfect for gift-giving whether it's Christmas or anytime, year round.

Quick Chocolate Fudge

¼ cup unsalted butter or margarine

3 squares (1 ounce each) unsweetened chocolate

1 pound confectioners' sugar

⅓ cup dry nonfat milk powder

½ cup light corn syrup

1 tablespoon water

1 teaspoon vanilla extract

½ cup chopped nuts

Melt butter and chocolate over boiling water. Sift sugar and dry nonfat milk powder together and set aside. Stir corn syrup, water, and vanilla into chocolate mixture over boiling water. Stir in dry ingredients in three or more additions, blending well after each addition. Remove from water and stir in nuts. Spread in buttered 8-inch-square pan and let stand until firm. Cut in squares.

Makes about 1¾ pounds.

Kneaded Chocolate Fudge

2 tablespoons unsalted butter or margarine
2 squares (1 ounce each) unsweetened chocolate
1 cup milk
3 cups sugar
¼ cup honey
⅛ teaspoon salt
1 teaspoon white vinegar
1 teaspoon vanilla extract
½ cup chopped nuts

Melt butter and chocolate in milk in large heavy saucepan. Beat to blend. Add sugar, honey, and salt. Bring to boil, cover, and boil 2 minutes. Uncover and cook *without stirring* until a small amount of mixture dropped in cold water forms a soft ball (240° F. on candy thermometer). Remove from heat and add vinegar. Cool to lukewarm, then add vanilla. With wooden spoon or balloon whisk beat until mixture thickens and loses its gloss. Add nuts and turn out on greased plate. Let stand until cool.

Knead 4 to 5 minutes. With lightly greased hands shape in 2 rolls about 2 inches in diameter. Wrap in wax paper and store in cool place until ready to serve or give. Cut in slices.

Makes about 2 pounds.

Christmas Fudge

⅔ cup (1 small can) undiluted evaporated milk

2 tablespoons unsalted butter or margarine

1⅓ cups sugar

½ teaspoon salt

2 cups (4 ounces) miniature marshmallows

1½ cups (9 ounces) semisweet chocolate pieces

½ cup chopped pistachio nuts

¼ cup crushed peppermint candy canes

Mix first 4 ingredients in saucepan. Bring to boil and cook 4 to 5 minutes, stirring constantly. (Begin timing when mixture bubbles.) Remove from heat and add next 3 ingredients. Stir briskly until marshmallows are melted. Pour into buttered 8-inch-square pan and sprinkle with candy. Cool thoroughly and cut in squares.

Makes about 2 pounds.

Old-Fashioned Chocolate-Nut Fudge

2 squares (1 ounce each) unsweetened chocolate

¾ cup milk

1 tablespoon light corn syrup

2 cups sugar

Dash of salt

2 tablespoons unsalted butter or margarine

1 teaspoon vanilla extract

1 cup coarsely chopped walnuts or pecans

Combine chocolate and milk in heavy 2-quart saucepan. Put over low heat and cook, stirring, until smooth and blended. Add corn syrup, sugar, and salt, and stir until sugar is dissolved and mixture boils. Continue boiling, without stirring, to 234° F. on a candy thermometer, or until small amount of mixture forms a soft ball when dropped in very cold water. Remove from heat. Add butter and vanilla and cool, without stirring, to 110° F., or lukewarm. Add nuts and beat until mixture begins to thicken and loses its gloss. Turn at once into buttered 8 x 4-inch loaf pan. Cool at room temperature until firm, then cut in squares.

Makes 18 pieces.

Cream-Cheese Fudge

2 packages (3 ounces each) cream cheese, softened

2 tablespoons cream or milk

4 cups confectioners' sugar

4 squares (1 ounce each) unsweetened chocolate, melted

1 teaspoon vanilla extract

1 teaspoon rum

Dash of salt

1½ cups chopped pecans or walnuts, divided

Beat cheese and cream until smooth. Gradually beat in sugar, then blend in chocolate. Stir in vanilla, rum, salt, and 1 cup nuts. Press into lightly greased, 8-inch-square pan. Cover top with remaining nuts. Mark in 64 pieces about 1-inch square and chill until firm enough to cut (about 15 minutes).

Makes 1 pound.

Sour-Cream Chocolate Fudge

2 cups granulated sugar
1 cup confectioners' sugar
1 cup sour cream
3 squares (1 ounce each) unsweetened chocolate
¼ teaspoon salt
1 tablespoon unsalted butter or margarine
1 teaspoon vanilla extract
1 cup chopped nuts

Mix first 5 ingredients in heavy saucepan. Bring to boil, stirring occasionally. Reduce heat and cook, without stirring, until small amount of mixture forms a soft ball when dropped in very cold water (234° F. on a candy thermometer). Add butter and vanilla, and cool to lukewarm. Add nuts and heat until mixture is thick and loses its gloss. Pour into buttered 9-inch-square pan. Let stand until firm, then cut in squares.
    Makes about 1¾ pounds.

Mocha Fudge

¾ cup evaporated milk
3 tablespoons instant coffee
2½ cups sugar
1 jar (7½ ounces) marshmallow cream
¼ cup unsalted butter or margarine
1 package (12 ounces) semisweet chocolate pieces (2 cups)
1 teaspoon vanilla extract

In 3-quart saucepan heat evaporated milk and stir in coffee to dissolve. Stir in sugar, marshmallow cream, and butter. Bring to boil, stirring constantly, and boil gently over medium heat 7 minutes. Beat in chocolate and vanilla until well blended. Pour into greased 8-inch-square pan. When cool, cut in 1- or 2-inch squares with sharp pointed knife rinsed frequently in hot water.

Makes about 1 pound.

Peanut-Butter Chocolate Fudge Pinwheels

1 cup (6 ounces) peanut-butter-flavored chips

1 can (14 ounces) sweetened condensed milk, divided

1 package (6 ounces) semisweet chocolate pieces (1 cup)

1 teaspoon vanilla extract

½ cup chocolate sprinkles

In medium saucepan over low heat, cook peanut-butter chips with half the condensed milk (about ⅔ cup), stirring occasionally, just until smooth. Remove from heat. Line a cookie sheet with foil; lightly grease a 12 x 10-inch area. With metal spatula spread peanut-butter mixture evenly to cover greased rectangle. When mixture cools slightly, pat gently with hands to distribute more evenly. Let cool 30 minutes.

In clean saucepan cook chocolate with remaining condensed milk over low heat until melted and smooth. Remove from heat. Stir in vanilla; cool slightly. Spread evenly over peanut-butter layer; let cool 30 minutes.

Lifting long side of foil, gently roll both layers together, jelly-roll fashion. Roll log in chocolate sprinkles, pressing gently so sprinkles adhere. (Do not handle too long or chocolate will melt.) Wrap tightly in plastic wrap. Store in cool place up to 2 weeks. Bring to room temperature before cutting in ¼-inch-thick slices.

Makes 48.

Double-Chocolate Cherry Bourbon Balls

These sinfully delicious chocolate confections are best after several days' storage.

> 1 package (6 ounces) semisweet chocolate pieces (1 cup)
> 3 tablespoons corn syrup
> ½ cup bourbon (see Note)
> 1 package (8½ ounces) chocolate wafers, crushed (2¼ cups)
> 1 cup finely chopped nuts
> ½ cup confectioners' sugar
> ¼ cup finely chopped candied red cherries
> Granulated sugar

In top of double boiler or bowl set over hot (not boiling) water, melt chocolate. Remove from heat; stir in corn syrup and bourbon. In large bowl mix well wafer crumbs, nuts, confectioners' sugar, and cherries. Add chocolate mixture; stir until blended. Let stand 30 minutes. Shape in 1-inch balls; roll in granulated sugar.

Makes 54.

Note: Ginger ale can be substituted for bourbon.

Daiquiri Balls

1 package semisweet chocolate pieces (1 cup)

½ cup sour cream

½ pound vanilla wafers

1 cup confectioners' sugar, plus extra for dusting

¼ teaspoon salt

3 tablespoons cocoa

1 tablespoon each grated lemon rind and grated orange rind

2½ tablespoons lemon juice

1½ tablespoons maple syrup

¼ cup rum

1 cup finely chopped pecans

Melt chocolate over hot water; cool. Add sour cream and refrigerate overnight. Form into balls, using ½ teaspoon of mixture for each. These will be used as centers.

Crush wafers; add 1 cup sugar, salt, cocoa, and fruit rinds. Add lemon juice, maple syrup, rum, and pecans, and mix together well. Form balls the size of walnuts around the chocolate centers.

Roll in confectioners' sugar. Store in airtight container.

Makes about 54.

Chocolate-Coated Prune-Nut Balls

½ pound pitted prunes

1 can or bag (7 ounces) or 2 cans (3⅓ ounces each)
    flaked coconut

2 cups coarsely broken walnuts or pecans

¾ cup sweetened condensed milk (not evaporated)

Grated rind of 1 small orange

8 squares (1 ounce each) semisweet chocolate

¼ cup unsalted butter

Mock Pistachio Nuts (optional)

Foil candy cups (optional)

Force first 3 ingredients through coarse blade of food chopper. Stir in condensed milk and orange rind, then shape in ¾-inch balls. Melt chocolate and butter in top part of double boiler over hot water. Holding each ball on fork, dip in chocolate mixture. Drain off excess, sprinkle with nuts, if desired, and put in foil cups; or set on jelly-roll pan lined with wax paper. Refrigerate until firm. For gift-giving, arrange in single layer in boxes and keep refrigerated.

Makes about 60.

Mock Pistachio Nuts

In small bowl, mix 5 drops yellow food coloring, 2 drops green food coloring, and ½ teaspoon water. Add ⅓ cup finely chopped walnuts, pecans, or almonds. Toss well to distribute color evenly, then spread on paper towel to dry.

Rich Chocolate Caramels

1 cup granulated sugar

1 cup brown sugar, firmly packed

½ cup light corn syrup

½ cup half-and-half

2 squares (1 ounce each) unsweetened chocolate

2 tablespoons unsalted butter or margarine, cut in pieces

1 teaspoon vanilla extract

Place sugars, corn syrup, half-and-half, and chocolate in large heavy saucepan. Bring to boil, stirring to melt chocolate and dissolve sugar. Reduce heat to moderate and continue cooking, stirring occasionally, until syrup reaches 248° F. on candy thermometer (firm-ball stage). Remove from heat. Quickly stir in butter and vanilla just until blended and butter melts. Pour into well-greased 8-inch-square pan. Cool; cut in small squares. If desired, top each square with pecan half or almond slivers. Wrap individually in plastic wrap or foil. Store in cool, dry place.

Makes about 1½ pounds.

Chocolate-Walnut Crunch

1 pound unsalted butter (2 cups)
2 cups sugar
¼ cup water
2 tablespoons light corn syrup
2 cups coarsely chopped walnuts
1 package (6 ounces) semisweet chocolate pieces (1 cup)
½ cup finely chopped walnuts

Melt butter over low heat in 1-quart saucepan. Add sugar and stir until sugar is melted. Add water and corn syrup. Continue cooking over low heat, without stirring, until a small amount of mixture becomes brittle when dropped in very cold water (290° F. on a candy thermometer). (This takes about 45 minutes.) Remove from heat and stir in coarsely chopped walnuts. Spread in buttered 15 x 10 x 1-inch pan and let stand until firm. Melt chocolate over hot water and spread evenly on candy. Sprinkle with finely chopped walnuts. Let stand until chocolate is firm; break in pieces.

Makes about 2 pounds.

Chocolate Fondant

2 cups sugar
2 tablespoons light corn syrup
½ cup water
2 squares (1 ounce each) unsweetened chocolate,
    melted and cooled
18 pecan halves
3 ounces white chocolate

In medium-sized deep saucepan mix sugar, corn syrup, and water. Bring to boil over medium heat, stirring to dissolve sugar. When boiling, wash sugar crystals from side of pan with pastry brush dipped in water. Set candy thermometer in pan and boil syrup without stirring to 242° F. (firm-ball stage).

Rinse large platter in cold water but do not dry. Pour syrup on platter but do not scrape pan. Let stand 5 minutes or until surface feels just warm, moving platter a few times to cool surface. Work candy with spatula or wooden spoon, scraping to center of platter, until white and firm. Scrape from platter into heavy or doubled plastic bag. Add melted unsweetened chocolate. Close bag and knead until candy is well mixed, smooth, and clings together. Shape in 1-inch balls. Press pecan halves into half the balls.

To coat remaining balls, melt white chocolate in small saucepan over very low heat, stirring occasionally. (Do not overheat or chocolate will separate). Spear fondant balls on fork and dip into white chocolate. Tap fork against rim of pan to knock off excess chocolate. Place balls on wax paper to cool.

Store fondant airtight in cool, dry place. Keeps about 1 month.

Makes about 36.

Chocolate-Nut Brittle

2 cups sugar

1 cup light corn syrup

½ cup water

1 teaspoon salt

2 tablespoons unsalted butter

3 squares (1 ounce each) unsweetened chocolate

1 teaspoon baking soda

2 teaspoons vanilla extract

2 cups peanuts

In heavy 3-quart saucepan over medium heat bring to boil sugar, corn syrup, water, salt, and margarine, stirring constantly. Then cook *without stirring* to hard-crack stage (300° F. on candy thermometer). Remove from heat. Quickly stir in chocolate, then soda, vanilla, and peanuts. Turn into greased 15 x 10 x 1-inch jelly-roll pan; with greased spatula spread to cover pan. Cool. Turn out of pan onto paper. With mallet break in irregular pieces.

Makes about 2 pounds.

Marbled Divinity

½ cup light corn syrup
2½ cups sugar
¼ teaspoon salt
½ cup water
2 egg whites
1 teaspoon vanilla extract
½ cup (3 ounces) semisweet chocolate pieces
Whole filberts

In saucepan mix first 4 ingredients. Cook, stirring, until sugar is dissolved. Cook without stirring, until a small amount of mixture forms a firm ball when dropped in very cold water (248° F. on a candy thermometer). Beat egg whites until stiff. Pour about half the syrup slowly over whites, beating constantly. Cook remainder until a small amount forms hard threads in very cold water (272° F.). Add slowly to first mixture and beat until very stiff. Add vanilla and gently fold in chocolate to give a marbleized effect. Cool slightly, shape in balls, and put on wax paper. Top each with a filbert and let stand until firm.

Makes about 1 pound.

Note: If preferred, drop mixture by teaspoonfuls into bonbon cups instead of shaping in balls. Or fill pastry bag with mixture, press out in even pieces, and shape in balls.

Chocolate-Rum Confections

8 squares (1 ounce each) semisweet chocolate

1 cup confectioners' sugar, lightly spooned into cup

1 egg

½ cup golden raisins

1 tablespoon dark rum or thawed undiluted
    orange-juice concentrate

About ¾ cup finely chopped pecans

In large heavy saucepan over very low heat partially melt chocolate. Remove from heat. Beat with wooden spoon until melted and smooth. Beat in sugar and egg just until smooth. Stir in raisins and rum. Chill mixture until firm enough to handle, 20 or 30 minutes.

Using 1 level teaspoon for each, pack firmly in ½-inch balls. (If candy seems dry, moisten hands to shape balls.) Press pecans firmly onto balls. (For easier coating, first brush balls lightly with corn syrup, beaten egg white, or water, then coat with pecans.) Store airtight in a cool, dry place.

Makes about 60.

Chocolate-Chip Meringues

2 egg whites
⅛ teaspoon salt
½ cup sugar
1 teaspoon vanilla extract
1 package (6 ounces) semisweet chocolate pieces (1 cup)

In small bowl of mixer at high speed beat egg whites with salt until stiff but not dry. Add sugar 2 tablespoons at a time, beating well after each addition (mixture should be very stiff and glossy). Stir in vanilla and fold in chocolate. Drop by teaspoonfuls 2 inches apart on ungreased cookie sheet.

Bake in preheated 300° F. oven about 25 minutes, or until light golden and firm to the touch. Remove to rack to cool. Good as is or with chocolate ice cream. Store tightly covered in a cool, dry place.

Makes about 24.

Double-Almond Toffee

1 pound unsalted butter

2½ cups sugar

1½ cups whole unblanched almonds

1½ cups semisweet chocolate pieces, divided

1½ cups lightly toasted chopped almonds

In large heavy skillet, melt butter and add sugar. Cook, stirring, over highest heat until mixture foams vigorously. Reduce heat to low and cook, stirring, 5 minutes longer. Add almonds, increase heat to high and cook, stirring, until nuts begin to pop. Reduce heat and cook, stirring, 7 minutes. (If mixture darkens too quickly, remove from heat but stir the full 7 minutes.)

Pour into 15 x 10 x 1-inch jelly-roll pan, and cool. Melt half the chocolate over hot water, spread over candy, and sprinkle with half the chopped almonds; cool.

Flip cooled candy sheet out of pan. Melt remaining chocolate and spread over other side of candy; sprinkle with remaining almonds. When cool, break in pieces. Store in covered metal container lined with wax paper.

Makes 3 pounds.

Chocolate Popcorn

2 quarts freshly popped corn

1 cup sugar

6 tablespoons corn syrup

¼ teaspoon salt

⅔ cup water

2 squares (1 ounce each) unsweetened chocolate

2 tablespoons unsalted butter or margarine

Put popcorn in large bowl.

In heavy saucepan mix sugar, corn syrup, salt, and water. Stirring, bring to boil. Cook without stirring to firm-ball stage (242° F. on candy thermometer).

Meanwhile, melt chocolate and butter together. Stir into hot syrup; pour over corn. Mix well, then turn out on greased cookie sheet. Cool, then break in clusters, or let stand until cool enough to handle. Then, with buttered hands, shape in 2½-inch balls.

Makes 12.

A Few Sauces
and Drinks

Included in this section is a selection of sauces for making a chocolate treat out of any dessert. Drizzle, pour, or flood your favorite ice cream sundae with the best ever Rich Hot-Fudge Sauce. Then store it for future indulging!

A mugful of foamy, frothy Hot Chocolate is the only thing to sip after a day of ice skating or snowball fighting. Or try a cup of Hot Brazilian-Style Chocolate, a classic drink filled with exciting flavors, perfect for a party.

Basic Hot-Fudge Sauce

4 tablespoons unsalted butter

4 squares (1 ounce each) unsweetened chocolate

⅔ cup hot water

2 cups sugar

¼ cup light corn syrup

¼ teaspoon salt

2 teaspoons vanilla extract

Melt butter in heavy saucepan over low heat. Add chocolate and let melt. Stir in water, sugar, corn syrup, and salt. Bring to boil over medium heat and cook without stirring until sauce is thickened, dark, and glossy, about 8 minutes. Remove from heat and stir in vanilla. Serve hot over ice cream.

Makes 2 cups.

Note: Sauce can be made ahead, covered, and refrigerated. Reheat in heavy saucepan over very low heat, adding 1 to 2 tablespoons hot water if sauce becomes grainy.

Rich Hot-Fudge Sauce

⅓ cup unsalted butter or margarine

2 squares (1 ounce each) unsweetened chocolate

2 squares (1 ounce each) semisweet chocolate

1 cup sugar

1 cup heavy cream

⅛ teaspoon salt

2 teaspoons vanilla extract

In large heavy saucepan melt butter and chocolates over very low heat. Blend in sugar, cream, and salt. Stir over low heat until hot and sugar is dissolved, about 5 minutes. Remove from heat; stir in vanilla. Serve warm.

Makes about 2⅓ cups.

Note: Store any leftover sauce, covered, in refrigerator. To serve, stir over very low heat until hot, adding a little water if too thick or grainy.

Chocolate-Orange Sauce

2 envelopes no-melt unsweetened chocolate,
    or 2 squares (1 ounce each) unsweetened chocolate

½ cup orange juice

1 cup sugar

Put chocolate in saucepan, and melt if squares are used. Stir in orange juice. Gradually add sugar and bring to boil. Good warm on sherbet or ice cream. Keep refrigerated.
    Makes about 1 cup.

Rich Raisin-Fudge Sundae Sauce

½ cup seedless raisins

¼ cup toasted slivered almonds

¼ cup unsalted butter or margarine

1½ squares (1½ ounces) unsweetened chocolate

¼ cup unsweetened cocoa powder

¾ cup sugar

⅔ cup heavy cream

⅛ teaspoon salt

1 teaspoon vanilla extract

Chop raisins and almonds coarsely. Melt butter and chocolate in heavy saucepan over low heat. Stir in cocoa, sugar, cream, and salt. Bring slowly to boil without stirring. Remove from heat and add vanilla, raisins, and almonds. Serve warm or cool on ice cream, plain cake, or pudding.
    Makes about 1½ cups.

Multipurpose Chocolate Syrup

Use as a base for beverages or toppings.

> 1 cup cocoa
> 1½ cups sugar
> ¼ teaspoon salt
> 1 cup boiling water
> 1 teaspoon vanilla extract

In heavy saucepan mix cocoa, sugar, and salt. Gradually stir in water; stir over medium heat about 8 minutes, or until smooth, shiny, and slightly thickened. Remove from heat; stir in vanilla. Store covered in refrigerator.

Makes 2 cups.

Quick Hot or Cold Chocolate Milk

For each cup of hot or cold milk beat in 1 to 2 tablespoons syrup.

Hot Chocolate

> 2 squares (1 ounce each) unsweetened chocolate
> 3 tablespoons sugar
> ⅛ teaspoon salt
> 1 cup boiling water
> 3 cups milk, scalded

Place chocolate in top of double boiler and melt over hot, not boiling, water. Stir in sugar, salt, and boiling water and blend thoroughly. Stir in hot milk and heat until very hot, beating with whisk. (If desired, whirl in blender.) Pour into mugs.

Makes 6 servings.

Hot Brazilian-Style Chocolate

Milk
Chocolate syrup
Grated orange peel
Almond extract
Cinnamon stick

In heavy saucepan, for each cup of milk add 2 to 3 tablespoons chocolate syrup, ½ teaspoon grated orange peel, 1 drop almond extract. Bring to boil over medium heat, stirring constantly. Before serving, beat with rotary beater until frothy. Serve with a cinnamon stick in each cup.

Chocolate-Banana Shake

1 ripe banana, cut in chunks
1 cup ice water
¼ cup chocolate syrup
¼ cup nonfat dry milk powder
3 ice cubes

Whirl all ingredients in blender until blended and ice has melted. Pour into 2 tall glasses. Serve at once.

Chocolate-Peppermint Flip

½ cup quick chocolate-flavored beverage mix
⅓ cup marshmallow cream
3½ cups milk
¼ teaspoon peppermint extract

Put all ingredients in blender and whirl until well mixed. Or mix first 2 ingredients, gradually add milk and extract, and shake vigorously.
    Makes about 4 cups.

Guatemalan Chocolate

2 squares (1 ounce each) unsweetened chocolate

2 tablespoons water

½ cup sugar

1 tablespoon cornstarch

2 cups freshly brewed strong black coffee

1½ teaspoons cinnamon

½ teaspoon vanilla extract

⅛ teaspoon salt

3 cups hot milk

Grate chocolate into top part of double boiler over boiling water. Add water and mix to a smooth paste; add sugar mixed with cornstarch; gradually stir in coffee. Beat until smooth. Cook for about 5 minutes, stirring occasionally. Stir in cinnamon, vanilla, salt, and milk. Blend thoroughly. Cook mixture about 20 minutes, stirring occasionally. Before serving, beat with rotary beater until frothy.

Makes about 6 cups, or 6 to 8 servings.

Note: This chocolate is also very good iced. Chilled, it has the consistency of a milk shake and can be served as a dessert drink, with a topping of sweetened whipped cream.

Spanish Egg Chocolate

2 squares (1 ounce each) unsweetened chocolate

2 cups milk

½ cup sugar

1 teaspoon vanilla extract

⅛ teaspoon ground cloves

1 egg

In top part of double boiler over hot water melt together chocolate and milk. Beat with rotary beater until blended. Stir in sugar, vanilla, and cloves. Beat egg until frothy in pitcher in which chocolate will be served. Pour chocolate over egg and beat again to a froth. Serve at once.

Makes about 3½ cups or 4 servings.

Index